SEE DO REPEAT

THE PRACTICE OF ENTREPRENEURSHIP

REBECCA J. WHITE, PHD

Permission requests:

> For permission requests, email Dr. Rebecca White at: books@drrebeccawhite.com with 'Attention: SDR Guidebook Permissions Coordinator' in the subject line.

Ordering information:

> Individual or small batch sales: Available via book retailers or through the author's website at: see-do-repeat.com

> Quantity sales: Special discounts are available for bulk purchases by corporations, associations, and other organizations. Visit see-do-repeat.com for details.

Digital presence and AI partner:

> Moonshot OS for Authors (moonshot-os.com/for-authors)

First edition printed in 2021. Updated edition 2024.

ISBN: 979-8-9919650-2-6 (hardcover)
ISBN: 979-8-9919650-0-2 (paperback)
ISBN: 979-8-9919650-4-0 (ebook)
ISBN: 979-8-9919650-3-3 (audiobook)

In loving memory of my mother, Betty White,
who first taught me the practice of entrepreneurship,
and to my family and students, who remind me
every day of the power of this practice.

"The difference between ordinary and extraordinary is practice."

—Vladimir Horowitz

CONTENTS

PART I: SEEING

PART II: DOING

PART III: REPEATING

FOREWORD

By Michael Houlihan and Bonnie Harvey

Founders of Barefoot Wine and Business Audio Theatre, New York Times Bestselling Authors, Top 5 2020 Business Audio Book Producer, Advisors, Teachers, Trainers, Keynote Speakers, and Avid Hikers.

What kind of a person would give up a 9 to5 for a 5 to9? What kind of a person would choose to be their own worst boss? Who would be willing to give up paid vacations and personal time off, or exchange the security of a paycheck for the anxiety of a cashflow projection?

That type of person we call an "entrepreneur." These folks recognize an opportunity, jump on it, and see it through. They believe they can mitigate the risks involved in bringing ideation to monetization - regardless of the setbacks. Using faith in their idea and persistence to bring it into reality, they push on, learning from their mistakes and never taking "no" for an answer.

In the West, and especially the United States, the term "entrepreneur" has a certain heroic and bigger-than-life connotation. But in much of the rest of the world, an entrepreneur is someone who couldn't hold down a job, and now is forced to create one for themselves. They may be looked down upon or seen as a disgrace to their family. If their first venture is not successful, the doom and dread of being a failure will hang over their heads for the rest of their lives.

Meanwhile, in the United States we celebrate these courageous risk takers with television shows, magazines, and websites. We here in the States understand that an entrepreneur learns valuable lessons from every experience, be it a "success" or a "failure." To us, they are like invincible superheroes!

Entrepreneurs have been elevated and adulated to the point that they appear to always have had the confidence and skills necessary to succeed. What we may not realize is that they too had to overcome self-doubt, inadequate training, misconceptions, and an abundance of seemingly insurmountable challenges.

In the past two decades, schools of entrepreneurship have popped up all over the country, supercharged by the Technological Revolution, the Great Recession, the Pandemic, and Climate Change. Opportunities abound, but how do you recognize them, how do you take action, and how do you keep going in the face of roadblocks and setbacks?

Nobody ever said being an entrepreneur is an easy task. But the road to success is made less daunting by hearing the mistakes made and lessons learned by successful entrepreneurs - and not just the superstars that we've all heard about, but the regular everyday folks whose success stories may never reach the headlines.

Rebecca White has heard hundreds of such stories. She is the entrepreneurial daughter of an entrepreneurial mother and became an entrepreneurial educator. She has interviewed hundreds of entrepreneurs and used her teaching skills to distill, amplify, and present the essential aspects of each story to inspire, motivate, and educate those of us looking for proven tools to help us succeed. In a word, she makes entrepreneurship look "doable."

After we wrote our own entrepreneurial success story, *The Barefoot Spirit*, and it became a New York Times Best Seller, we shared our experiences with students around the world at more than 60 schools that teach entrepreneurship. Everywhere we spoke, the students had basically the same two questions:

"How do you prepare for the unknown?" and, "How do you keep going when you run up against a wall?"

We love these questions! They are sincere and from the heart, and they come from people who have identified the two biggest challenges entrepreneurs face. Rebecca has identified the answers.

Sure, the brand we created, Barefoot Wine, eventually became the world's largest wine brand. But did you know that we started it in the laundry room of a rented farmhouse with no money and no knowledge of our industry?

We loved what we were doing, but also suffered many setbacks that almost killed us and the brand. We had to reject many popularly-held misconceptions and focus on the tough realities of business and refine our entrepreneurial mindset. We had to learn and apply what we learned quickly.

Many of the setbacks we had could have been avoided if we had had the insight encapsulated here in Rebecca's book. This is an essential handbook and road guide for anyone serious about achieving entrepreneurial success. After all, it *is* doable!

PREFACE

This book is a tribute to Betty White, the woman who was not only my mother but also my first entrepreneurship teacher. Yes, my mom was Betty White. While she was not the Betty White of celebrity fame, she was an equally interesting woman, who spent her life as an artist, business owner, mom, and inspiration, to most everyone she met.

At a time when few women chose a career and family, my mom raised two children, while she owned and ran a successful business venture. In a small rural town in West Virginia, where most women did not call attention to themselves, she was a business owner, an artist who was painting nudes, and a jogger, before anyone else knew what that meant (she would frequently get the offer of a ride by people passing by). She was a woman who spoke her mind, baked her own bread, made yogurt, and grew bean sprouts. Mostly my mom was interested in the world, everyone and everything in it. And she is a person who lived life with gusto.

My mother enjoyed life immensely, as a mother, artist, creator, and entrepreneur. She was a gentle and sweet soul, a spirited fighter who staunchly defended her family and loved ones, and a true innovator—always ahead of her time. She not only pursued her own passions throughout her life, but she was also my greatest cheerleader and supporter while I was pursuing my own entrepreneurial dreams.

A few years ago, after eighty-nine years of a full and productive life, my mother succumbed to a long illness. When she died, someone gave me a beautiful poem. It reminded me that even though she is not physically with me every day, she still lives on in the lessons she taught me through the life she lived. My mom was the first person I came to know in the world and as it turns out she had an entrepreneurial mindset through which she viewed the world. And, not surprisingly, I have lived my life studying and practicing my own brand of entrepreneurship.

My mother was an artist and business owner. She loved learning and took great joy in being a creator. I, too, have applied entrepreneurship to every job I've had and to the creation of my own business ventures. The mindset she taught me, which hopefully I have passed on to my children and now grandchildren, is one of possibility, while embracing all life has to offer. It is one of curiosity and of personal responsibility and always considering how one individual can make a difference. It is a life that embraces and celebrates the learning which comes from failure. It is one of always knowing that you have a safe harbor in family and friends who can help you through the dark times when failure hurts so much.

My motive for writing this book is to pay tribute to my mom and share some stories of the amazing entrepreneurs I have met. It is also the next evolution in my own entrepreneurial journey. I have been blessed with so many teachers along the way, and I want to pass that on. Whether you were born into a family where you learned an entrepreneurial mindset, or it is one you wish to develop, my hope for you is that this book can help you advance your practice of entrepreneurship and realize your own entrepreneurial dreams.

INTRODUCTION

Entrepreneurship is a way of life. Like yoga or meditation, entrepreneurship is not about perfection; it is about transformation and change through practice. A business founder may build and create a very successful business, but make no mistake, they never stop learning. Similarly, entrepreneurship is a journey. Have you ever noticed that when entrepreneurs talk about what they have done, they love to tell their "story?" It is usually one that involves hard work, challenge, failure, and perseverance. It is also one where they have learned a great deal, and most entrepreneurs love to share what they have learned.

Early in my working life, I struggled with finding my vocational path. I changed my college major many times, and after graduating worked in numerous businesses, from banking to an engineering firm. Later, I decided to go back for an MBA, thinking I would work in the corporate world. But life intervened, and I got married. We moved to a small town, and I found myself teaching at the small college I had attended as an undergraduate. After several years of teaching, and with two babies in tow, I decided to pursue my PhD. It was shortly after finishing that I was introduced to the field of entrepreneurship as an academic discipline.

I had taken a position at a state university in the Midwest. Knowing my background in a family business and my personal interest in business startups, my department chair invited me to create and offer a course in small business. The small class of only fifteen students soon turned into a thriving program which gained national status and ranking, and I became immersed in the world of entrepreneurship education.

I had found a way to apply my own entrepreneurial mindset to an academic career. Over the past three decades, I have had the opportunity to help build several such programs. I've been a part of the educational journey of thousands of students, participated in interesting research projects, and provided training and consulting services to firms ranging from small businesses to public companies. I have even taken time away from the academic community to start several of my own businesses.

During the past thirty years, the field of entrepreneurship education has exploded into what might even be thought of as a global movement, as courses in entrepreneurship have grown exponentially worldwide. Once a topic offered in a class or two on a handful of campuses, entrepreneurship is now one of the most popular college degrees available. It is a topic of a wide variety of community-based education programs on a regular basis. While most entrepreneurship courses and programs had their roots in business colleges, courses and even entire degree programs can now be found in most colleges across campus from the sciences and agriculture to the arts and medicine.

Participating in this development and growth of an academic discipline has given me a unique perspective on the field, and an opportunity to leave my own imprint. My colleagues and I have participated as scholars firsthand in advancing the field as it has moved from teaching about how to start and manage a small business to a discipline that bridges a wide variety of topics from business to design to psychology. Now entrepreneurship is not just about how to start a business, it is about starting a new venture in most any context. It is about a way of seeing and acting that is based in opportunities and possibilities. Students who study entrepreneurship today are learning about a mindset. In most cases, they are also learning by doing. Experiential education, now popular in many business fields, has been a mainstay in entrepreneurship education for many years.

About twelve years ago, I began to develop some concerns about the direction of our discipline. Although the field had gained immense popularity and had begun to develop science around how to teach entrepreneurship, the content in the field remained quite fuzzy. The concept of an entrepreneurial mindset was not clearly defined. It was not clear how to assess learning nor what one should expect of an entrepreneurship graduate. If we are teaching mindset, does it still make sense to judge our graduates on whether they start a for-profit business, how many people they employ, and whether they can raise venture funds? While these are all great indicators of success, was it also a success when one of our students launched a new product or developed a new process in their corporate job or at their church? I decided to dig into mindset a bit more, with the goal of figuring out not only what we should be teaching but also how we can measure learning.

While the origins of the concept date back to the early twentieth-century work of Austrian economist Joseph Schumpeter and others, it was a mere twenty years ago that Professors Rita McGrath and Ian MacMillan, popularized the concept in their book, *The Entrepreneurial Mindset*. Since that time, many have tried to clarify this perspective and there are many theories and opinions about what it means to look at the world through an entrepreneurial lens.

My own contemplation on mindset began with the review of an essay written more than a hundred years ago by James Allen. Produced as an easy-to-read-and-digest self-help book, Allen's main thesis was about thought and the impact of thought on intention and behavior. He suggested that our thoughts will dictate our actions, so we need to be guardians of thought. Working from this basic premise, I began to dig into the work on mental maps. One analogy resonated with me. If you want to find a location in New York, you can't use a map of Chicago. The idea that our actions are dictated by our thoughts and we form mental maps that guide our behavior, made a lot of sense to me. Learning how to shape mindset required an even deeper look at how mindset is developed and transformed.

My research on mindset led me to the work of Stanford Professor Carol S. Dweck, who popularized research on the concept of mindset and its role in human behavior.[1] Mindset is made of deep-seated beliefs that govern our lives, our choices, and our behavior every day. It is made up of all our assumptions about the world around us and about ourselves and others. Developing mindset begins at birth and changes over time. For some, mindset changes dramatically over their lives while others maintain a more fixed mindset throughout life. Changing mindset is transformational and challenging. It often occurs from interventions and life experiences but may also come from introspection and personal motivation.

The relationship between mindset and behavior is complex and multidimensional. Mindset drives behavior. However, changes in behavior can also impact mindset. In fact, changing mindset often begins with changes in behavior. Some call this "acting as if." However, simply changing behavior is also not enough. We can't *do* our way out of a thinking problem. As Einstein said, "We can't solve a problem with the same thinking we used to create it." Mindset is deeply personal, and changes must come from within.

As I began to apply what I was learning to my work as an educator, I quickly recognized each learner came to me with their own personal mindset, which they had been working on their entire lives. Some of them came with a mindset that was firmly established and perhaps even entrepreneurial; after all, they were attracted to the field for some reason. Others would come with varying degrees of an entrepreneurial mindset. This meant, for learning to be transformational, it must be customized and be experiential. I had to find solutions to three remaining questions: What is the mental map of an entrepreneur? How is it developed? And how can this process of learning be customized and experiential?

Answering these questions meant clarifying what made the mindset of an entrepreneur different from non-entrepreneurs.

It also meant I needed to dig into the science of teaching and learning. About this time, I was introduced to competency-based education (CBE) by my friend and colleague Dr. Kevin Moore. Kevin was a co-founder of a consulting company that combines the science of teaching and learning with technology to provide technology-based education programs for a wide variety of organizations. I quickly saw that the application of CBE in entrepreneurship may provide an answer to these questions.

Introduced by David McClelland in the early 1970s, competencies were recognized as significant predictors of employee performance and success and were traditionally more associated with training than education. However, in recent years more advanced education systems have come to value it as a framework for designing and implementing education that focuses on the desired performance capabilities of the learner within this broad definitional context.[2] Whereas traditional education tends to focus on what and how learners are taught, CBE is focused on whether or not learners can demonstrate application of learning to solve problems, communicate effectively, perform procedures, and make appropriate decisions within a given context. CBE was a fit because it not only addressed teaching, learning, and assessment, it is also based in a deep understanding of the abilities, skills, and behaviors of successful performers.

The starting point, for developing any competency education model, is to understand the underlying factors that lead to successful application. In this case, how do entrepreneurs think and act? To do this, it was important to study hundreds of entrepreneurs to see if competencies would emerge. I needed to collect hundreds of stories. To do this, I didn't want to depend upon the stories of the 1%—the superstar entrepreneur stories that are told repeatedly. I wanted to get the stories of the other 99%—the everyday entrepreneurs that make a difference but whose stories are not often shared on a wide scale. Because this is where most of my students and clients would be. This process of talking to entrepreneurs[3] and figuring out what really differentiated them started with a very long list of competencies; however, through hundreds of interviews with everyday entrepreneurs, some very exciting findings began to emerge.

First, despite the uniqueness of their entrepreneurial endeavors, there was a common mindset driving their choices. Second, while they all depended upon a common set of abilities and skills to develop these competencies, when they didn't possess a necessary skill or ability, they sought it out in someone else who could help them. Third, and perhaps even more exciting to note, the more they developed their mindset, the more likely they would attract others who could fill in those gaps. The interviews began to tell a story of mindset, intention, and attraction. From this work, the three competencies began to emerge. These three competencies then provided a model for creating a learning path for the experience and practice of entrepreneurship, which I could share with my students and clients:

- the ability to recognize entrepreneurial opportunities (SEE)
- the willingness to act on them (DO)
- the resilience to execute past failure (REPEAT)

Having a model and a language was a start, but there was still the question of how to share the model and how to help others learn this practice. I already knew experiential education was the answer, but I needed to better understand the cognitive processes of learning. As I talked to these entrepreneurs and pieced together their stories, something simple yet profound began to crystalize in my data. The See, Do, Repeat model was not just a set of competencies and skills required for any entrepreneurial endeavor. They are also the customized, experiential pathway to gaining those skills and the entrepreneurial mindset.

To fully understand how this works, we must consider what is often referred to as competency structures or the architecture of a competency-based learning model. This architecture is built by first identifying the primary competencies required for a specific task or job. For each competency, skills and abilities are identified. The learner is then asked to provide some evidence of skill or ability in three ways—which are hierarchical from a learning perspective—knowledge, application, and mastery.

From birth, we have all learned by seeing, doing, and repeating. When we learned to walk, we saw our parents and siblings walking, so we tried it and we kept trying it until we got the hang of it. We fell, but we were determined and so we accomplished our goal. Walking was the competency we, and the grown-ups around us, wanted. Standing up, balancing, learning to put one foot in front of the other were the skills we learned. Repeated practice allowed us to gain mastery of walking. We saw, we did, and we repeated until we learned to walk.

Competency-based learning doesn't require mastery. That is why it is such a beautiful model for entrepreneurship education. Instead, it is a model that can be used as a reminder of what is important and where to focus our learning. A well-designed competency structure becomes a model for what to prioritize in learning to reach a specified outcome. Remember, entrepreneurship is practice, and like yoga or meditation, the goal is not mastery. The goal is showing up each day. It is unlikely any of us will fully master each of the three competencies in the See, Do, Repeat model on any given day or with respect to any given endeavor. In fact, my research and experience has taught me mastery of all of these is not important. There are other ways, which I will share, to reach tremendous success without mastering all of these. What is important is having a focused practice.

The elegance of the See, Do, Repeat model for the practice of entrepreneurship is that it describes both what to know and how to learn it. While entrepreneurship is never easy or simple, having a focused way to develop your entrepreneurial practice can be extremely valuable. In fact, having a curated approach, which can be integrated into everyday life and work, may be the only way someone who is working 24/7 on an entrepreneurial venture can take the time to improve their practice.

To help you build this practice into your life as quickly and as effectively as possible, this book has been organized into three parts: Seeing (Opportunity Recognition), Doing (Taking Action), and Repeating (Executing Past Failure). Each part includes three chapters, each focusing on a required skill. At the beginning of each chapter, you will find some reflection questions—sort of a pre-test—to help you figure out where you are on the pathway of learning. At the end of each chapter, you will find a learning guide which is also divided into three stages of learning—See (Knowledge), Do (Application), and Repeat (Mastery)—to help you continue your own customized learning program. I encourage you to begin your practice now by turning to the next page.

PART I
SEEING

CHAPTER 1

OPPORTUNITY

There is a tide in the affairs of men.
Which taken at the flood, leads on to fortune;
Omitted, all the voyage of their life
Is bound in shallows and in miseries.
On such a full sea we are now afloat.
—Julius Caesar, Act-IV, Scene III, Lines 218–224

Entrepreneurship is opportunity centered: it begins with an opportunity and exists only when there is an opportunity. Entrepreneurship is open to those who can see an opportunity, act on it, and execute past failure, the people who can *see, do,* and *repeat.* But because it is opportunity centered, the ability to recognize a feasible and impactful opportunity is vital to the entire process.

If you are reading this book, it is likely you either want to pursue an opportunity now or in the future or you are already doing so. In the first part of this book, we will examine entrepreneurial opportunities, define them, and discuss how we know whether they are both impactful and feasible. Later, we will talk about how to be successful in that pursuit. But for now, let's take a minute and assess your concept. How many of the following questions can you answer with a "yes?"

- Are you passionate about your opportunity?
- Does your opportunity provide significant value to your customers?
- Is this the right time to pursue your opportunity?
- Can you make money on this opportunity?
- Will others who invest time or other resources into my opportunity be rewarded?

How did you do? If you were able to answer "yes" to all five of these, you may have an entrepreneurial opportunity, but keep in mind there are still more questions to address before you decide for sure. If you couldn't answer "yes" to all of these, don't despair, that is where this book comes in. Every new venture, whether it is a business, a new product or service, a new organization, or not-for-profit group, starts with a thought. An idea that must be shaped and molded into feasible and impactful entrepreneurial opportunities. Let's get started on yours.

OPPORTUNITY DEFINED

The word *opportunity* stems from Latin origin: *ob* (toward) and *portus* (port). The original term *op-port-tu* referred to the time, before ports were dredged, when the captain and crew had to wait for the tide to rise to go into the ports. Sailors used the phrase *ob portus* to denote the best combination of wind, current, and tide to sail to port. However, the only way to seize such weather conditions was if the vessel's captain had already sighted the port of destination. Knowing the weather conditions without knowing the destination was useless. Therefore, a ship was in a state of *opportunitas* when its captain had decided where to go and knew how to get there.

I met Edouard "Ed" Carrie, a young student from Haiti, when I walked into my first class on the campus of the University of Tampa. Even after many years of teaching, I was nervous about meeting this new group of students. Arriving a few minutes before class to review notes, I was standing at the podium when Ed approached. He reached out a hand to me and with great enthusiasm said, "Dr. White, we are so excited to have you here. We have been waiting for you!" Talk about pressure. I had just met one of the most motivated student entrepreneurs I had ever encountered. He had a tremendous passion for entrepreneurship, and he was anxious to learn from everyone and everything he experienced.

Over the course of the next year, Ed was a constant fixture in my office and an enthusiastic student in class. Ed was an entrepreneurial soul in search of an opportunity. He had the passion, the willingness to take action, and, with a father who led and owned a business, had the encouragement of his family to be an entrepreneur. Each time I saw Ed, he had a different idea. He wanted to pursue all the typical "student ideas" like having a T-shirt screen printing business. Exasperated with his constant ideas, one day I reminded Ed of one of my favorite lines for students in this search phase, "If you want to find an opportunity, look for a problem." Like so many of the wonderful students I have the honor of working with, although Ed envisioned himself as an entrepreneur, he hadn't experienced enough of life and hadn't yet done the work to see a real problem.

It wasn't until he went home for the holidays his senior year and experienced a life-changing event that he found what would ultimately lead to his entrepreneurial journey. On the afternoon of January 12, 2010, a magnitude 7.0 earthquake struck the island of Haiti. Sadly, this disaster was one more misfortune in a country that had suffered decades of political, economic, and social setbacks. Ed was home on the holiday break, and he emailed me to say he may be late coming back. Ultimately, he was able to come back and when he did, he returned with his entrepreneurial passion. During the next semester, his final one at the university, he designed a company that would ultimately become the first professionally managed company to collect trash, in a country that was overrun not only by debris from the earthquake but from decades without trash collection and disposal systems. The company not only provided a venue for cleaning up much of the country, but it also provided an income to thousands of Haitians.

CRITERIA OF AN ENTREPRENEURIAL OPPORTUNITY

While every opportunity begins with an idea, an opportunity is much more than a conceptional combination of thoughts. It is a unique combination of the thinker (in this case the entrepreneur) and the environment (or economic marketplace). Entrepreneurial opportunities, the subject of this book, are those situations in which new goods, services, raw materials, and organizing methods can be introduced and sold at greater than their cost of production.[4] Those worth pursuing are a complex mix of timing combined with personal experience and goals. An opportunity that might have worked well last year may very well not succeed today. Similarly, an opportunity that is right for me may not work for you. Opportunities emerge at the intersection of the entrepreneur and their environment.

There are four essential qualities of an entrepreneurial opportunity: It must be *interesting and attractive* for the entrepreneur, it must be *timely*, it must have *financial benefit* for all those who invest time, talent, or treasure, in the business and it must *add value* for the customer.

For Ed Carrie, the experience of a major weather event disaster in his home country helped him identify an entrepreneurial opportunity that he found interesting and worth pursuing. It was clearly timely and needed. But he wasn't so sure the concept would be financially beneficial or if he had the skill set needed to

> DO
> Opportunities emerge at the intersection of the entrepreneur and their environment.
> REPEAT
> SEE

create a company that could add real value for the customer. He needed to do some more work to figure this out.

Ed's initial idea for his company was to recycle the concrete that had literally filled up the communities in Haiti after the earthquake. But interactions with another classmate led to a significant change in the plan. Ed had a classmate whose father owned a waste management company in the northeastern US. Ed was invited to intern with their company after graduation. During this work experience, Ed learned more about the industry, and with that knowledge (as well as a favorable agreement to acquire machinery needed), he returned to Haiti to start the company with a new business model.

Through his new strategy, Ed was able to provide value in several ways. First, his company provided an organized way to clean up a country, which had historically lacked trash removal and disposal systems. Second, thousands of unemployed Haitians were able to live on the money they could earn by collecting and bringing in plastics and paper they found around their homes and neighborhoods. He also found a way to monetize the business. At that time there was a significant market globally to sell recycled plastics. Ed had created an entrepreneurial opportunity. A business he found interesting and worthwhile, that provided value, was timely, and could generate revenue and make the effort financially worthwhile.

Like Ed, Lisa Druxman found her entrepreneurial opportunity after experiencing a major life-changing event. Lisa is the founder and CEO of Fit4Mom, the nation's leading company for pre- and postnatal health, wellness, and fitness programs for motherhood. Lisa was passionate about fitness and had spent time working in the fitness field when she learned she was pregnant with her first child. In search of a workout buddy in her hometown of San Diego, California, she soon learned there wasn't a strong community of women in a similar situation. To fill that need as well as her desire to work with more personal control over her time as a new mom, she started her company.

Lisa didn't start out to be an entrepreneur. She simply had a personal need. But she soon found out she was only one of thousands of women who had the same need. Her passion turned out to be an entrepreneurial opportunity. It was timely, filled a market need, and could be financially viable through a franchising model. Today Lisa and Fit4Mom have created opportunities for women nationwide, with 300 franchises and 2,600 locations around the world.

For many entrepreneurs, like Ed and Lisa, the identification of an entrepreneurial opportunity will surface after experiencing a life-changing event. For others, the emergence will take many years.

Donna Salyers is the founder and CEO of a faux fur manufacturing and direct seller business in Covington, Kentucky. I met Donna when I was living and working in the Greater Cincinnati area. As a young woman, Donna loved to sew. One day she grew frustrated with the sewing column in the local newspaper and decided to write a letter to voice her disappointment about their content. The paper wrote back and invited her to be a contributing editor. As she tells it, they told her, "If you can do better, why don't you write for us?" She saw this as an opportunity, took them up on the offer, and began her career in a sewing-related field.

The column led to writing a series of books on sewing. In the early 1980s, the Cincinnati communications company E. W. Scripps expanded from newspapers to cable TV, and Donna saw another opportunity and created and starred in a cable TV show about sewing.

Donna's career as an expert in the sewing industry began to grow, and over time, she was invited to New York for an interview about sewing programs. It was winter and Donna decided she wanted a fur coat to wear to the city. However, as she was driving to the store to buy her coat, she heard a short story about the abuse of animals to produce fur coats. She decided she couldn't contribute to that problem, so she would make her own fake fur coat. She did, and when she went to New York for her interview, her new coat got rave reviews. This led to the start of Donna Salyers Fabulous-Furs. With customers in forty-six countries and sold by Neiman Marcus, Saks Fifth Avenue, Nordstrom, Gorsuch, and other luxury boutiques and hotels throughout the country, Donna's business is now one of the leading faux fur brands in the world.

While Donna's entrepreneurial opportunity was based on her passion, she didn't start her company as soon as she recognized her interest in sewing. Unlike Ed and Lisa, the timing wasn't quite right yet. She began by building her knowledge as well as her network, but along the way, she recognized the changes in the marketplace and took advantage of them. Moving from newspapers to cable TV was the first transition in her story. She also saw trends in the marketplace very early regarding animal rights.

When Donna first started her faux fur company, she was selling sewing kits for her coats. She would purchase the material, create packages of sized pre-cut material, and then sell them via mail orders and on the phone. One day she got a call from someone who represented the actress, Loretta Swit (if you are old enough, you may remember her as Major Margaret "Hot Lips" Houlihan on *M*A*S*H*). Loretta had heard about her coats and wanted to purchase one. Donna didn't respond that she sold kits, not coats. Donna said, "Yes" and that she would pass this along to the "ready-to-wear" department. Turns out, the ready-to-wear department was Donna and her sister in the basement making a coat for Loretta. Donna had gotten the message that there was a customer need for her products and Fabulous-Furs was born.

Donna's big entrepreneurial opportunity began with a passion for sewing and by pursuing that passion, over time the market and customers emerged. What made the difference for Donna was that she was astute enough to recognize *when* to pursue her business. Like the captain at the helm of the ship, when the conditions and the tide were high, she headed to port. Donna was able to bring together the needed elements of a business that would be interesting, timely, provide value to customers, and make money.

TAKING THE FIRST STEP TO ENTREPRENEURSHIP

The ability to recognize an opportunity, which is interesting, timely, financially viable, and adds value, is the starting point for the creation of any new venture. It is the first step in the See, Do, Repeat practice of entrepreneurship, so getting this right is critical to everything else. The good news is that this is a skill that can be learned, practiced, and applied by anyone.

Ed, Donna, and Lisa are just three of thousands of similar entrepreneurial stories. From the builders of big corporations to the freelancer, the solo entrepreneur, employees working within a larger company (often known as intrapreneurship), to those in not-for-profit organizations, the requirements of an entrepreneurial opportunity are the same: to find a meaningful pursuit that is timely and provides value to the customer and to those invested in the venture.

The recognition of an entrepreneurial opportunity begins with the unique perspective, interests, and experiences of the entrepreneur. Like Donna's sewing interest, Ed's experience with the earthquake in Haiti, and Lisa's new experience of motherhood, the recognition of an opportunity comes from a passion or interest developed from experience. Sometimes that experience is a pleasant one (like a sewing hobby) or an unpleasant one (like a damaging earthquake). Either way, life provides us with many sources of inspiration for entrepreneurial opportunities.

But passion is not enough. The environment and the willingness of the entrepreneur, to learn and act on that learning, also dictates whether an idea is an entrepreneurial opportunity. In the next two chapters, we will examine

The good news is that this is a skill that can be learned, practiced, and applied by anyone.

DO · SEE · REPEAT

ways to improve your odds of recognizing viable entrepreneurial opportunities. As with any competency, there are skills, abilities, and behaviors that can help you master opportunity recognition. But before we look more deeply into those, take some time to prepare by practicing the skills associated with opportunity recognition.

PRACTICE: OPPORTUNITIES

SEE

Opportunity recognition is about connections, but oftentimes we need to disconnect to connect. The ability to recognize opportunities begins with awareness. So many times, we live our lives on auto pilot and we miss much of what is going on in the world. Taking time to disconnect from our electronics and our own busy mind can give us the chance to begin to *see* differently. How many opportunities are right in front of you but go unnoticed because you are not paying attention? Consider driving to work using a different route this week or taking a walk in a different part of your neighborhood or city. What did you notice? Did you see something that you had never noticed? Were you surprised by anything? Now try talking to someone and really listening to them. Ask questions and get to know someone on a deeper level. Find out more about them. Did you learn something new? Maybe you found a new connection.

DO

Make a "bug list." This is a list of as many things you can think of that bother you. What is frustrating? What makes your life or your work harder or more challenging? Now, look at the world. What bugs you about the greater world around you? Where do you see problems? Make the list as long as you can. How many did you write down? Now try to add more. Push harder. Maybe you are someone who never complains, so you aren't bothered by many things. Or maybe you see lots of ways for improvement. Either way, can you push yourself and see if you can come up with twenty-five, fifty, or even more items on your bug list?

REPEAT

Review your bug list. Were you able to see lots of different and unique problems or were many of them a variation on the same problem? If so, try again and see if you can stretch your mind to find more. Now can you think back to what you saw on your walk or drive, or what you learned in your conversations when you were practicing more awareness? Can you begin to see connections which might lead to opportunities you never considered? Keep pushing. Try to see if you can find at least three to five new ideas you never considered that could have the potential to be an opportunity. Something *interesting* to you, *timely*, has *financial potential*, and could provide a potential *valuable solution* to the problem. Write down your ideas in a notebook or journal, so you can return to them later. Make it a practice to evaluate your opportunities this way.

CHAPTER 2

DISCOVERING AND CREATING OPPORTUNITIES

To have entrepreneurship you must first have entrepreneurial opportunities.

—Shane and Venkatraman, 2000[5]

Have you ever noticed how some people seem to always find great opportunities? After years of research on opportunity recognition and of interviewing and working with hundreds of successful entrepreneurs, I have found that the ability to recognize an opportunity is a skill that can be learned and practiced by anyone. In fact, becoming a master at recognizing opportunities requires a few exercises, which are simple, yet often hard to practice. Those people who seem able to magically find all the great opportunities have simply made a practice of the requirements. You may even already be practicing some of them yourself. How many of the following statements are true for you?

- I am curious and interested in the world around me.
- I take the time to learn something new.
- I like to travel and explore the world.
- I like to learn about a lot of different topics.
- I have researched my opportunity and know as much as possible about it.
- I am good at finding connections between totally unrelated items.
- I spend time reflecting on what I see and learn about.
- I routinely disconnect from work and my responsibilities.

RECOGNIZING ENTREPRENEURIAL OPPORTUNITIES

Kevin Harrington, one of the original sharks on the popular *Shark Tank* TV show, grew up in Cincinnati, Ohio, and from an early age, he loved to talk with his father about business. As a young boy, he loved the idea of selling. By his early teens, he had already created a successful driveway sealing business. Later, Kevin would recognize the power of television and late-night TV. He leveraged this knowledge to become known as the inventor of the infomercial, a pioneer of the "As Seen on TV" brand, and the brains behind commercializing thousands of today's popular brands and inventions.

Kevin's mantra, "But wait there's more," doesn't just apply to his sales strategy, it applies to his life. He continues to innovate and help others do the same. Kevin embodies the entrepreneurial mindset, and his life has been and continues to be about the recognition of opportunities. When I talked with Kevin on the *EnFactor Podcast*, he credited his curiosity and his willingness to embrace and learn from failure as key factors in his ability to recognize thousands of opportunities over the years.

Research has shown the ability to recognize opportunities involves a variety of behaviors, from pattern recognition and an ability to connect the dots, to intuition, to alertness, and to situational awareness. Experimentation and learning are essential to the process. Recognizing opportunities requires curiosity, failure, and a willingness to explore new ideas, concepts, and cultures. However, knowing these kinds of behaviors will lead to the recognition of new opportunities and applying them in a consistent manner to generate viable entrepreneurial opportunities are not the same. I have found in helping my students and my clients build opportunity recognition skills over the years it has been important to put all these behaviors into a system, which can be practiced and developed over time. To understand the system, let's take a look at how we came to what we know about the recognition of entrepreneurial opportunities.

Perspectives on the identification of entrepreneurial opportunities have their roots in the research of economists who, from the early twentieth century, were trying to explain the role of the entrepreneur in the financial system. This research suggests there are two different, but not mutually exclusive, pathways to access a viable opportunity.[6] As early as 1934, in an attempt to explain the origin and concept of entrepreneurial profits, the Austrian born economist Joseph Schumpeter[7] suggested the role of the entrepreneur in the marketplace is one of being a creator of new solutions to customer problems, which are inherently an improvement over the previous way. He named this phenomenon, *creative destruction*.[8] According to Schumpeter, entrepreneurs are constantly finding new and improved ways to fill the needs of customers and in doing so the new product or service destroys the former, less effective one. This is the classic definition of innovation, which we closely associate with invention and the entrepreneurs that dramatically change the way we work, live, and do business.

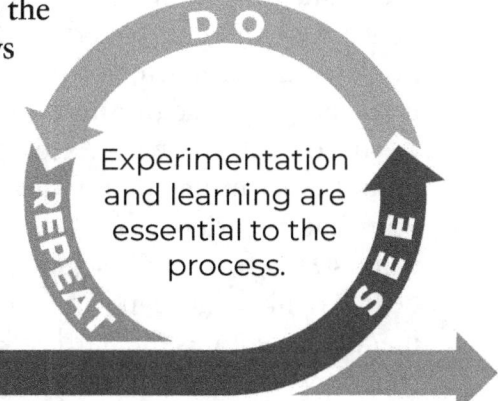

Experimentation and learning are essential to the process.

About forty years later, an American-born economist Israel Kizner, who also closely identified with the Austrian school of economic thought, suggested a second pathway.[9] While Kizner is thought to have agreed with Schumpeter regarding the entrepreneur's role in innovation, he also suggested a business founder may discover an opportunity that already exists in the market. He understood the market often has gaps or inefficiencies, and the astute and alert entrepreneur might see a way to better meet the needs of customers.

Whether you are creating an entirely new market or discovering a way to improve on a current product or service, there is a process that can help you find the perfect mix of market need and product solution, which most people don't fully understand. The method was first outlined in 1926 by the British psychologist Graham Wallas and decades later was expanded upon by an American advertising executive James Webb Young in his brief book *A Technique for Producing Ideas*. Webb outlined a simple to understand, but often hard to put into practice, five-step process that I use in my classes. The book begins with an introduction from the author about his motivation for writing the book. According to the author:

> This has brought me to the conclusion that the production of ideas is as definite a process as the production of Fords; that the production of ideas, too, runs on an assembly line; that in this production the mind follows an operative technique which can be learned and controlled; and that its effective use is just as much a matter of practice in the technique as is the effective use of any tool.
>
> If you ask me why I am willing to give away the valuable formula of this discovery I will confide to you that experience has taught me two things about it: First, the formula is so simple to state that few who hear it really believe in it. Second, while simple to state, it actually requires the hardest kind of intellectual work to follow, so that not all who accept it use it.

Thus, I broadcast this formula with no real fear of glutting the market in which I make my living.

A METHOD FOR CREATING AND DISCOVERING OPPORTUNITIES

STEP 1: COLLECTING RAW MATERIAL

The first step in this process is to *collect raw material* with which to work. Any new concept or creative solution starts as an idea. What is an idea? An idea might be defined as a mental impression. The word has it roots in the Greek term *idein,* meaning "to see," and later *idea,* meaning "form or pattern." An idea is indeed a mental impression, but the source of an idea is the process of combining elements.

According to Webb Young, any new idea is simply a combination of existing ideas that are a novel combination. The ability to connect ideas, or to connect the dots, is foundational to the process of creative problem-solving. In fact, research[10] has suggested, the ability to connect the dots is one of the key skills entrepreneurs use to identify business opportunities. And, as Webb Young points out, "The habit of mind which leads to a search for relationships between facts becomes of the highest importance in the production of ideas." In other words, in order to generate an idea, there must be dots to connect. The dots are the raw material for the formation of a pattern or an idea.

Collecting raw material is about conducting research. Like my students, you may be thinking at this point that doing the research for a business concept or to solve a problem is a given and there isn't anything new and interesting in this idea. But this is where Webb Young's work is so fascinating. He points out there are two kinds of raw material: *general* and *specific.* When we conduct research to solve a problem, we often focus on finding information that is specific to the problem. So, if you plan to start a catering business, you do the business and market research to determine whether it makes sense.

This is what Ed Carrie did for all his business ideas. Certainly, this is important, however, this kind of research usually serves only to identify the questions which must be answered and addressed. But, if you want a creative solution, you must also gather *general* material—that is, information about the world around you. In most cases, the collection of this general data will precede the collection of specific data. For example, before Ed knew he needed to conduct research on the business of recycling, he needed to understand and experience the conditions in Haiti. Once he understood the context and the problem, he then could begin to dig into the process of learning about recycling.

To be effective and efficient at generating creative solutions, you must make collecting general material a *habit,* so you have more "dots" to connect. That is, in order to generate creative solutions, you need to look outside of the information specific to your problem, and it must become something you do on a regular basis. Therefore, curious people are often more likely to be prolific idea generators. They are interested in the world around them, and they are constantly collecting raw material with which to work.

Fortunately, becoming more proficient in creative problem solving is available to anyone. The process requires being present and applying what we might call a beginner's mind. Reading something every day that is not on your normal reading list is a great place to start. Try to replace even fifteen minutes of your time on social media, regular news feeds, or TV shows with reading that challenges the way you view the world. One of the greatest obstacles most of us have with this is we tend to limit our reading to material that supports our opinion. What if you were willing to open your mind to consider something that challenges your beliefs?

Another way to gather raw material is to listen. When you talk to others, ask more questions and listen with true curiosity. Traveling or learning a new skill or hobby is another way to gather raw material. When I met my husband, he introduced me to the world of boating and, specifically, to sailing. I had limited experience with boating and zero experience with sailing. Learning all the new terminology and the skills associated with this new hobby was a challenge, to say the least. But because I was willing to put in the time and learn, I not only have many memorable and fun experiences with family and friends, but I have also been able to translate what I learned into my work in both business and education.

Reading, listening, traveling, and hobbies are just a few of the ways you can increase the raw material that will feed your creative decision-making practice. I encourage you to expand on these and find your own methods. To get started, create an *entrepreneurial practice journal* and take notes or draw pictures of what you are learning. You can use this journal as you move through the creative process and as you work through this book.

STEP 2: MENTAL MASTICATION

The process of building a puzzle is a great analogy for the second step in the creative problem-solving process. When I talked with Benson Riseman, co-founder of Green Dot, the company that brought us the first prepaid debit card, about his thoughts on recognizing opportunities, he used the building of a puzzle to describe the process. According to Benson, when we first open a puzzle box and see all those tiny pieces, we may get overwhelmed and think the job is too great to tackle, or we may think we are missing something because we don't immediately see how everything fits. But if we just start, find the edge pieces, or figure out a color strategy and begin to look for ways to connect the pieces, with patience, they will come together. This is the process where we mentally chew on the data we have collected in the first step. It is where we make connections and find relationships. It is more abstract than the first stage of gathering raw material, because as Webb Young suggests, "It goes on entirely in your head."

During the mental digestion process, there are three phases. Like a puzzle, you start by putting together the pieces that are easy (like the edges and matching large sections of colors in a puzzle). These are the obvious connections. When you are working in this phase of the process, write these down. No matter how incomplete, jot them down in your journal. At this point, when I assign this to my students, most of them think they have finished the assignment because they don't see any more obvious relationships. But once we talk in class, they begin to see they are still early in the process, and this is where the second phase of the mental digestion process begins. You too may want to stop once you have a long list of connections, but I encourage you to keep going.

With practice, the mind has the capability to go well beyond the obvious. However, like working a puzzle, when you are training the mind, you may need to call on a few techniques to keep the process moving forward. To facilitate the second phase, write down all the limits or boundaries you have put on your thinking. In other words, what do you believe about the problem you are trying to solve that you held constant throughout the first phase? Once you do that, remove those constraints or even state the opposite. Then, see if more relationships and connections emerge once you have removed or expanded the possible boundaries.[11] This second phase may yield some extreme possibilities and you may be tempted to dismiss them, but don't do so. Add these to your list and keep going.

You will know you have entered the third and final phase of the mental digestion process when you get to the point where you are circling back, are truly frustrated, and begin to question everything you have been working on

With practice, the mind has the capability to go well beyond the obvious.

up to this point. When you know you have really persisted in finding connections and relationships and your mind reaches a state of exhaustion with the entire process, it is time to set the entire project aside and move on to the next step in the creative process. But before we move on to the third stage, let's discuss how you can build the skill of mental mastication so the process becomes second nature.

Training the mind to find connections and relationships is like any other skill, it takes practice. But with practice, you can call up this process on demand and even speed it up. One fun technique you can use is to generate a list of novel applications for an ordinary item, like a flowerpot or a pencil. Create a practice of combining two unrelated ideas to generate something of value. Take a hobby and a new technology and see if you can find a way to connect them to solve a problem you have observed in your world.

In my graduate class on creative problem-solving, I give my students many assignments that require them to find connections. In one recent assignment, the task was to take the technology used in autonomous vehicles and apply it to an existing problem and generate a new product or market solution. One of the students in the class was an Olympic athlete from Mexico. At the time, he was training in Tampa by swimming in the Gulf of Mexico. One of the challenges he faced was that he had to look up periodically to see where he was headed and to make sure he did not have any obstacles in his path. However, looking up in this way slowed him down. His creative solution for the class assignment was an autonomous lead that could "swim" ahead of him. It would provide his course and notify him of obstacles, or even change course as needed. This student already had general information about swimming and training, and he also had personal experience. All this general material could then be combined to provide a novel idea and a creative solution to the specific problem.

STEP 3: INCUBATION

Over many years of practice, study, and teaching, I have come to believe the first two steps of gathering raw material and mental mastication are the foundation for success as a creative. Making these two processes a part of daily life can greatly enhance skills associated with finding creative and innovative solutions. Much like gardening, these steps are the planting of seeds that, when watered and left to grow, can yield tremendous results. But, as with the garden, the planting of seeds is not the end of the process; there is much more. In some ways, it is the third step of the process, that our data-rich, fast-paced world makes the most difficult for us.

After you have clearly defined your problem, gathered raw material, and considered potential ideas, connections, and solutions, you must then make a conscious effort to drop the project and put it out of your mind as completely as you can. At this point, you make no direct effort toward finding a solution, because remember, you have pushed your thinking on the subject as far as possible in the second step. Interestingly, this third step, the one where you stop working on the solution is, in some ways, one of the hardest for most people. Most of us want closure. We feel uncomfortable with uncertainty so having an answer, any answer, is sometimes preferred to getting the most creative and innovative answer. And this is especially true for entrepreneurs where there is often a sense of urgency and where impatience has been of great service to the entrepreneur's ability to get ahead of the competition and take advantage of changing markets. However, to truly find creative solutions, those that could lead to dramatic change and competitive advantage, this third step is required.

Routine breaks is one of the keys to deep cognitive efforts.

In fact, most of us have already experienced this step in our lives many times. For example, have you ever had the experience of losing something, like car keys, an important document, or household item, only to find it when you stop looking for it? If so, then you have experienced *incubation*, the process of letting go to allow the answer to emerge.

There is plenty of research which demonstrates that taking breaks from focused work can enhance outcomes. In fact, building in routine breaks is one of the keys to deep cognitive efforts. However, in this context, we are not talking about simply being lazy or taking a break from work to scan your social media. The goal is to create a break that is purposeful and restorative. For example, many studies have demonstrated the power of being immersed in nature. A 2008 study by a team of psychologists[12] shared the results of an experiment where subjects were split into two groups, one that took a walk in an arboretum and the other through the busy city center. The two groups were then asked to perform a challenging cognitive task. The researchers then switched the groups, having the group who first walked through the natural environment now walk through the busy city and the other group switch from the city walk to the arboretum walk. Each time, the group who spent time in the natural environment had the superior performance. This study, and others, confirmed we have a finite amount of directed attention and when it is exhausted, we will struggle to focus. The creative process requires that we give our minds a break.

As with the previous steps in the creative process, there is a way to enhance incubation. The key is to build rituals into your life to give you built-in incubation periods. When I talk to my students about this process, I tell them to find their "Zen." Zen is often associated with Zen Buddhism which aims at enlightenment through meditation. But we also use it to refer to a state of calm attentiveness, where your actions are guided by intuition rather than by conscious effort. We often find ourselves in this kind of state when we get lost in something we deeply enjoy. It can also happen when we take on a repetitive physical activity.

For some people, gardening and being in nature allows for this kind of meditative state. For others, it might be playing basketball or meditation. Over the years, I have learned I can restore my mind and body and my Zen while running or playing the piano. I often come back from running with the best ideas, as my mind has been free to roam during the repetitiveness of the activity. My husband often laughs about coming home to find me sitting at the piano bench with a laundry basket beside me, totally unaware I have lost hours at the piano bench with wrinkled laundry by my side. Where can you totally lose track of time and self? This is when your mind is free to restore your directed attention.

Research has shown building a ritual of restorative incubation is valuable to your health, and the bonus is that it can also enhance your creative problem-solving skills. Incubation might sound like an easy step and one most everyone would easily commit to practice. However, as I mentioned earlier, while most of us understand the value of this stage, we find it hard to commit to a practice of incubation because we are impatient and want to get to the solution, the answer, as quickly as possible.

Several decades ago, in his book *The Seven Habits of Highly Effective People,* Steven Covey outlined a life-changing theory of time management. In that book, he referenced what he called the "Law of the Farm." With this principle, he was explaining the difference between social and natural systems. According to Covey:

> In agriculture, we can easily see and agree that natural laws and principles govern the work and determine the harvest. But in social and corporate cultures, we somehow think we can dismiss natural processes, cheat the system, and still win the day.

But as Covey points out, while we might think we have found a way to shortcut the system and it may even work in the short-term, in the long run, the principles and laws of nature will rule. The same is true of the creative problem-solving process. Like the farm, if you want to build your creative problem-solving skills, you must respect and practice the principles that lead to the most innovative outcomes. The good news is, if you trust in the process and put in the time and effort, there is plenty of evidence this method works.

STEP 4: ILLUMINATION

We finally reach the stage of the process that begins to provide some closure. This is the stage the uninformed often believe to be the starting point of creative problem-solving. This is the stage we seek, the one we have been impatiently waiting to arrive. It is the magic I mentioned previously. It is the point where the proverbial light bulb shines. This is when we finally have the BIG IDEA! And the most interesting aspect of this stage may be that now the solution does indeed seem to have been there all along. This is the stage we call *illumination* because the solution, which was previously obscured by the massive information we have been processing, now seems obvious.

If you study the lives of great inventors, you will often find they have ritualized these first four stages of the creative problem-solving process into their lives. A few years ago I read *How to Think Like Leonardo da Vinci* by Michael Gelb. Born and living much of his life in and around Florence, Italy, da Vinci was a critical figure in the late Renaissance and arguably one of the most creative minds recorded in history. His contributions can be found not only in the arts and design (for which he is most often remembered) but also in engineering, math, the sciences, cartography, and much more. For example, he is credited with conceptually inventing many items we use today, such as the parachute, the helicopter, an armored fighting vehicle, the use of concentrated solar power, a calculator, a rudimentary theory of plate tectonics, and the paddle boat.

In his book about da Vinci, Gelb points to seven principles upon which da Vinci built his life. If you study these, from curiosity, experience, and strengthening your senses (Step 1), to embracing paradox and systems thinking (Step 2), to a logic/imagination and mind/body balance (Step 3), you will find these seven all support the process we have been discussing. Moreover, da Vinci is also credited with developing an interesting way of sleeping, known as the polyphasic sleep process or the "da Vinci Sleep Schedule." This approach to sleep allowed him to speed up the problem-solving process by interspersing his around-the-clock work with twenty-minute power naps. These naps provided frequent incubation (Step 3) that could then serve to initiate illumination (Step 4).

Of course, Leonardo da Vinci is perhaps extraordinary in terms of his vast creative contributions. But you don't have to look far to find many stories of this process at work in the lives of countless others. For example, Webb recounts a conversation he had with Frederic Eugene Ives, the inventor of the halftone process, a method of reproducing photographs on a printing press:

> While operating a photostereotype process in Ithaca I studied the problem of half-tone process [Step 1]. I went to bed one night in a state of brainfog over the problem [end of Step 2 and beginning of the Step 3] and the instant I woke in the morning [end of Step 3] saw before me, projected on the ceiling; the completely worked out process in operation.

As you consider building your own creative skills, I don't think it is necessary to change your sleep habits or adopt a totally different daily schedule; however, I do believe once you begin to understand this process, you may find you want to develop your own creative rituals. The result may well be the illumination of meaningful and valuable solutions to the problems and opportunities you encounter as an entrepreneur and in life.

As I mentioned earlier, the uninformed often believe illumination, this fourth step, is the entire practice of creativity. Now, hopefully, you would agree that is not the case and that there is a method of which the idea is only one element. However, it is important to point out, while there is a sense of euphoria and completion associated with the illumination of a potentially significant idea, there is one more very important activity to undertake. The final step is also the one that derails most people, because it involves not only acting on the idea but taking the time to get feedback from a specific group of people. But more about that in the next chapter. For now, just keep in mind this quote credited to the famous game inventor Nolan Bushnell, co-founder of Atari and founder of Chuck E. Cheese's Pizza Time Theatre chain:

> Everyone who's ever taken a shower has an idea. It's the person who gets out of the shower, dries off, and does something about it who makes a difference.

PRACTICE: IDEATION

SEE

Quantity of ideas improves the quality of ideas. This is one of the most important rules of ideation. Ideas come from everywhere. Our daily activities, our conversations, our travels, every experience and interaction we have can provide us with ideas that have the potential to become viable opportunities. Paying attention and learning to make connections will increase the number of ideas. But with ideation, it is not just about outcome. It is also about process. The goal of ideation is not only to generate ideas but to understand the process through which we arrived at those ideas. Understanding this process is important because it allows us to better evaluate and test the underlying assumptions we made to generate the basic idea. As you go through your day, consider the process of ideation. Pay attention. Reflect on the ideas that arise for you and begin to review and identify the process involved in getting to those ideas.

DO

Choose a time period to devote to test your creative problem-solving skills. For one day or even one hour in one day, *try paying attention.* During this time pay closer attention to the world and people around you. Make notes on what you are learning in your journal. At the end of the time period, see if anything you learned sparks enough of your interest and has the potential to become a viable opportunity. See if you can really *push your thinking* a bit further than usual. Write down what you are thinking. Then go to bed or do something that allows you to *relax* and to fully forget about what you have written. Go back the next day, or in several days, or even a week. When you look at what you wrote down, what did you find? Did the time away provide any *insights*?

REPEAT

How did the creative problem-solving experiment work for you? Did you generate lots of ideas, or did you struggle to come up with even one idea? Did the process lead to any meaningful insights or even opportunities? If so, that's great. If not, don't worry. The process will work but it works best when it becomes a habit. The process of creative problem-solving takes time and a certain amount of faith. To become a powerful ideator and increase the number of meaningful opportunities in your life, you must commit time and energy to the process. And you may need to make some changes in your life. Make the process a ritual. Try applying this to problems on a daily basis:

- Make awareness a habit. Can you expand your world and knowledge? Maybe you can learn something new, meet some new people, try a new hobby. Expanding your world doesn't require you to spend a lot of money or take an epic trip. It might just mean meeting your neighbors and spending time at the park. There are opportunities all around us. Do you consciously pay attention? When you travel or experience something new, are you truly exploring the world and people around you or are you mostly interested in getting the best photo so you can share it on social media? When you have a conversation with someone, are you listening and learning or are you spending your time thinking about what you are going to say? Are there some changes you can make to increase the input of *raw material* in your life?

- Carve out a time each day to writing down your ideas and connect them. Consider getting up twenty minutes earlier every day or taking twenty minutes at the end of the day to write. When you first start, don't judge your writing or your connections, just write. The discipline of journaling can be both therapeutic and empowering. Later, spend some time *thinking* about how to connect your ideas to problems to generate creative solutions. Push yourself. When you are really frustrated with the entire process, put it all aside and forget it.

- Make it a priority to find time each day to *relax* and forget about the problems you are trying to solve. Remember, this time is as important as the hard work time.

- Build in time periodically to reflect on what you have written, to see if you have any *insights*. Was there something you saw or someone you met last week who could help you with a problem you are facing today? What kind of connections can you make? What kind of opportunities do you find when you look back?

CHAPTER 3

CREATING VALUE

The most important thing is to just get started . . .
figure out what's valuable, put it in front of people
and if you're not embarrassed, you waited too long.

—Nicholas Hinrichsen, co-founder, Carlypso and WithClutch

A viable opportunity must create value for the customer. Without customers, all we have is an idea. Underlying feasibility and impact can create value for the people who buy and/or use our product. After putting the first four steps of the creative process to work, you may have identified what you believe is a viable solution. Until you have confirmation from the customer, you cannot yet be confident that your concept is ready. But this step also requires some action on your part. How many of the following are true?

- I have shared my opportunity with several people who have experience in my industry.
- I have shared my opportunity with people who are experienced entrepreneurs.

- I can describe my customer in detail and know them intimately.
- I interact frequently with the people who fit the profile of my customers.
- I have given customers the chance to try my product or service.
- I frequently solicit feedback from my customers.
- I have gotten negative feedback on my opportunity.
- I have had to change and modify my product or service to better create value.

THE PRIMACY OF CREATING VALUE

Entrepreneurship is about creating sustainable value for customers. An idea generated might gain tremendous traction with investors and might show some early promise and still not be able to create sustainable value. But it also doesn't mean the time spent in evaluating the concept is wasted. In fact, that time is some of the most valuable for an entrepreneur. This is the stage where there is significant learning and where your network will expand even more.

Consider the story of Nicholas Hinrichsen and Chris Coleman. After graduating from Stanford Business School in 2013, the two cofounded a company called Carlypso, a company like Amazon for cars. Afterward, they joined YCombinator, a business accelerator that helps promising companies get started by providing contacts and seed funding, which is

DO

Entrepreneurship is about creating sustainable value for customers.

REPEAT

SEE

funding at the earliest stages in the life of a business. During this time, Nicholas and Chris raised a total of ten million dollars in venture funding, took their service to market, and in 2017 sold to Carvana, currently the third largest used-car retailer in the US.

When I talked with Nicholas about his story, he shared his insights about navigating these early stages of testing and development with his business. He also confidently told me that Carlypso would have ultimately failed had they not combined efforts with Carvana. While Carlypso had some of the ingredients necessary for sustainable success, it also lacked some very important ones. Interestingly, he saw all of this as learning, which led him to his next startup, WithClutch.

In my graduate classes on innovation and creative problem-solving, my students read one of the classic books on the subject by Hungarian American psychologist Mihaly Csikszentmihalyi. Best known for his work on happiness and creativity, he is famous for recognizing and naming the psychological concept of flow, a state of highly focused and productive concentration that humans find enjoyable. While this concept of flow is fascinating, and we do spend class time discussing and considering this human condition and its role in life and creativity, one of my primary reasons for asking the students to read his work is so they can understand his perspective on forms of creative output and the role of experts in the process.

My students are often surprised by the assertion that there are two types of creativity. The first may be thought of as creativity, simply for the sake of creating. We may think of this kind of creativity as something akin to play. Children love to create. If we walked into a classroom of preschool-age children and asked how many of them can draw a picture or write a song or make up a story, most of them, with very little exception, would raise their hands and then, without much prompting, begin to sing, draw, or tell a story.

I used to play this game with my children in the car. When we had a long trip, we would collectively tell a story, each one of us adding to the content of the one before. It was a fun and interesting way to pass the time and, of course, the educator in me believed it was a great way for them to use their minds and develop their imagination. Children learn through this kind of creative play. And as adults, we can also find release and fulfillment through this kind of creativity.

Csikszentmihalyi, however, also points out there is a second form of creativity. While it can have many of the same elements of personal fulfillment, it must undergo the scrutiny of the field, in order to be a form of creativity that produces a value output. My students are often put off by this notion that some creative output has value while others don't. However, this is something every entrepreneur must learn. And this is where the final step in the creative problem-solving process becomes critical to the recognition of an entrepreneurial opportunity.

In the previous chapter, we discussed the first four steps in the creative problem-solving process: gathering raw material, mental mastication, incubation, and illumination. This process includes several important activities: adopting a curious and open mindset that leads to seeking out information, which is both specific to the problem and general in nature; using a journal to keep track of ideas and information gathered through the process; and finding ways to disconnect from the problem through exercise, meditation, or other activities that allow for an uncluttered mind. The work of these first three steps may then lead to the illumination of a meaningful solution.

While the goal of the creative problem-solving process is quite obviously to get to a solution, the "aha" moment is not the final step in this process. In fact, when the proverbial light bulb is illuminated, there are quite often many aspects of the solution that are hidden. As Webb Young points out, this stage "[m]ight be called the cold, gray dawn of the morning after. In this stage, you have to take your little idea out into the world of reality."[13] In other words, in order to ensure the solution is viable, it is critical that we get input. This is the fifth and final step of the creative problem-solving process and is often referred to as the *evaluation* stage.

With his work, Csikszentmihalyi is primarily focused on the creation of novel ideas. Not unlike Webb, he addresses the role of evaluation of ideas. In his definition of creative output, Csikszentmihalyi argues that an evaluation process, by experts in the field, is required in order to determine whether an idea is new and has application to a specific area. According to Csikszentmihalyi, "There is no way to know whether a thought is new except with reference to some standards, and there is no way to tell whether it is valuable until it passes social evaluation."[14]

It is vital to consider two necessary but distinct groups that are important in the recognition of an entrepreneurial opportunity. These two groups can save every entrepreneur significant time and help reduce the risk associated with entrepreneurship. The first and perhaps most important group is the customer. Based on his own personal experience and his research, Dr. Jeffry Timmons, one of my mentors and a pioneer in entrepreneurship education, developed guidelines for the new venture creation process I use with my students to measure the viability of entrepreneurial opportunity. First, a good idea is not an opportunity. Second, there must be a sizable and accessible market for the product. In other words, there must be enough people who want what you plan to offer and who are willing to spend their money on what you are selling. Third, there must be a sufficient difference between what it costs to produce or acquire the product or service and the price you can charge for it (also known as margin).

IDEAS ARE NOT OPPORTUNITIES

The first measure of an opportunity is to test whether your idea is worth continuing to evaluate. In my work, I always recommend nascent entrepreneurs follow the advice of Csikszentmihalyi and share their work with experts in the field. This is especially important if they don't have experience in the field themselves but is still valuable for anyone regardless of experience. However, I have seen that most of my students and the entrepreneurs with whom I work want to hold their ideas too close, fearing they will be stolen or criticized. Let's take a look at each of these concerns.

There are many stories of business ideas being stolen, and for this reason, entrepreneurs wait too long or totally fail to share their concept with the very people who can help them. In the movie *The Social Network*, the legal battle between Mark Zuckerberg and the Winklevoss brothers, who argued that Zuckerberg stole code from their concept (ConnectU) when he built Facebook, was detailed. If you followed the story, you know in the end, the judge ruled that the brothers were trying "to gain through litigation what they were unable to achieve in the marketplace." In other words, the idea is not what made Facebook successful. In most instances, the idea is just a tool in the hands of an entrepreneur. In fact, most ideas must go through a series of pivots and changes in order to be successful, and it is only in sharing the idea that those enhancements are recognized. Moreover, in most cases, it is the entrepreneur who has the most motivation and is the expert and, thus, much more capable of acting on the concept than an outsider.

On the other hand, for many of us, sharing our ideas with others can be very frightening and possibly painful. This is something I often see with novice entrepreneurs and students. Creators can begin to see the creation as an extension of themselves and when it is critiqued, can feel personally assaulted. I can recall this challenge with my own academic career. As a new PhD, my position as an educator was dependent upon not only being a good teacher but also on conducting research, developing theory, and publishing academic journal articles. In order to keep my job past the first few years, I had to show that I had research promise. This evidence that

DO · SEE · REPEAT

Ideas must go through a series of pivots and changes in order to be successful.

I was going to be a successful scholar was measured, in large part, by the number of peer-reviewed publications I was able to secure. Thus, my creative output had to be read and critiqued by the experts in my field. And even though I had a lot of input and feedback during my graduate programs from professors, it felt different when I was part of the field myself. I was a high achiever, and I didn't want to fail. I felt like I was supposed to be an expert; after all, I had the degree to prove it. But I also knew how little I really did know and how much I still had to learn. So, I held my work too close. And when I got negative feedback, instead of appreciating it as a pathway to improving my creative efforts, I took it too personally.

Over time I learned this approach did little to help me grow and it actually began to impede my progress toward my career goals. I learned to let go and appreciate feedback and begin to see possibilities that I couldn't see without expert input. What I learned in this process was that a good idea will actually expand with the right kind of input. But it was important that it was the right input, so I had to learn to share my work with those who knew the most about the subject of interest.

Besides a fear of theft or criticism, entrepreneurs can fall prey to another obstacle: too frequently entrepreneurs tend to fall in love with their idea too soon. All ideas that are up for consideration for a new business venture require intensive research and evaluation. However, once an idea is hatched and we have gotten even a little encouragement, the excitement of a prospective business venture can take over, and we lose our ability to seek out and hear feedback which doesn't align with our thinking. We fall in love with our concept. And, if we are in love with our work, we are not open to listening to feedback. Far too many entrepreneurs have fallen in love with their idea before they put it out for feedback, and when the flaws begin to emerge, they attempt to explain them away or ignore them and continue forward even in the face of reality. But ignoring negative feedback can be disastrous.

MARKETS: BIG AND AVAILABLE

Most people who decide to start a business know they must have customers. But what they fail to understand is the market must be large enough to sustain the business and it must be accessible and willing to spend enough of their hard-earned money on their product. Gaining clarity about whether there is a big and available market for a new venture is challenging. But there are methods that can help you answer these questions.

A market for a new venture can be thought of as having four primary characteristics. It is a group of people or businesses who have a need for the product or service offered, who have also the money needed to buy the product or service and are willing to spend it on what you want to sell. When I ask my students to define a market in this context, they usually get the first two but often don't include the last two. I remind them, if they need a car, they may want to buy a Porsche, but they may not have the funds, or if they do, they are likely to need to spend those funds on college tuition for now and not a Porsche (unless they are very fortunate).

In order to determine whether there is a market for your product or service, you need to start by identifying the market you believe is most likely to buy your product. This involves revisiting the problem you have identified and understanding who has that problem, and how they may be solving that problem now. It also includes clarifying which group of people or companies need your product or service. However, regardless of need, identifying this first market for your new venture requires a deep understanding of how they think and live and whether they have the financial ability and willingness to spend money on your product or service.

Most people think conducting market research is asking customers whether they would buy a product or service if it were available. While this form of market research may be useful in instances where the markets are well understood by the customer, classic market research often doesn't work when entrepreneurial opportunity is being evaluated. In fact, in most cases, while they might attempt to provide the best and most honest answer, prospective customers often don't even know whether they would buy an innovative or new product or service if you asked them. So, the results of classic market research often don't work for entrepreneurs. However, there are other models and methods, which have been proven to work for entrepreneurial opportunities. Let's look at each of these.

DESIGN METHODOLOGY

Design methodology, a form of problem-solving, developed fields, such as engineering, industrial design, and architecture, in the 1950s and '60s and includes a group of approaches to solving problems in a way that will improve the odds of creating and launching a business which has a meaningful market.[15] In his book *The Art of Innovation*, Tom Kelley, a partner at IDEO, a design and innovation consulting firm, outlines the five stages of their process. I have adapted the first four stages of their process for use with my students and clients to better clarify and meet market needs. Let's look at each of these.

The first step to evaluating the feasibility of an idea is to deeply understand the market, the technology, and the constraints you may face in the launch of your idea. This includes the research discussed in Chapter 2 as well as input from experts in the field discussed previously. It also includes an even deeper dive into the business environment.

In the first class in our entrepreneurship graduate program, a university reference librarian joins us to discuss how to conduct business research. We use what I call a funnel question approach. In order to assess the feasibility of any new business concept, it is important to answer a series of questions that begins broadly but narrows as you advance through the questions, allowing a deep dive into the context in which you will operate the prospective business. The funnel begins with a broad understanding of the economic, legal, and political environment. This may be on a global, country-specific, regional, state, and/or local basis. Of particular importance here is to understand the constraints and opportunities that you will likely face with your new venture. Next, it is important to understand the industry and competitive environment. Earlier in the opportunity discovery stage, you probably collected some information on the industry as part of the specific data gathering process. But at this point, your research needs to get even more specific, to include such information as the growth rate of the industry, the trends, and the factors driving change in the industry.

It is also important to learn everything you can about your competitors. This includes mapping them with respect to the benefits they offer their customers. There are many sources to find this kind of information that range from simple internet and library searches to trade associations. An easy starting point for industry and competitive research is to visit the North American Industry Classification System website to determine the primary industry in which you will operate and gather some basic information about the growth rate, trends, and competitors. From there you can begin to explore trade associations and talk to experts in the field.

While secondary research and interviewing and getting feedback and input from experts is necessary, it is not sufficient to determine viability. It is only the starting point because it fails to address the primary concern in the creation, design, or discovery of a viable market opportunity: customer experience. The next three steps provide that information.

Once you believe you have a clear understanding of the market, technology, and constraints, it is time to observe people in real-life situations, where they have needs that your product or service might address. This means not only talking to them but also taking an anthropological approach.

Several years ago, one of our student teams earned one of only six spots in the final round of the Hult Prize competition. This international competition is an annual, yearlong competition that challenges college students to identify an entrepreneurial opportunity. One that could not only generate a profit but also solve a pressing social issue such as education, food security, water, or energy.

Each year the prize committee names the problem and thousands of student teams compete for a one million dollar prize. That year the problem posed by the Hult Prize committee was to develop a business concept that could educate ten million children, from infancy to age six, living in urban slums. What set our students apart from the other 60,000 students who were competing in the competition was that our team selected a target location, Lagos, Nigeria. And they went there twice during the yearlong development of the concept to get to know the people and to learn what it means to live there. What they learned while they were in residence was everyone used cell phones. The mission of their final concept, Tembo, was to maximize human potential through education via mobile phones. By working with the providers of cell phone service in the area, they were able to establish a program, that not only used cell phones to provide content but also to incentivize parents to become early childhood educators of their children.[16] By spending time getting to know what it meant to live the life of their customer, they were able to develop a sincere empathy for them and create a product that would work.

But empathy for your customer today is not enough. It is also valuable to visualize how customers will use and interact with your concept today and in the future. A few years ago, I was hired to assist a company who owned and operated airport stores across the US. They were in the process of bidding on additional store space in the Hartsfield-Jackson Atlanta International Airport (ATL). In 2019 and 2020, ATL was reported to be the busiest airport in the world by passenger number and second busiest in aircraft movement. As you might guess, the retail spots in ATL were highly coveted spaces, and my client was very interested in offering an innovative concept during the bidding process. To help them address this task, we held a two-and-a-half-day off-site workshop and spent the time in a visualization process. The process provided the team with an opportunity to not only deeply consider the current traveler but also to begin to gain some clarity about the traveler of the future, by creating visual representations of that person from name, to demographics, to behavior, and travel lifestyle. After significant consideration and review of the options, the team preparing the bid was then able to build out a concept based on their visualization of the airport customer of the future.

In my classes, I also have my students create an archetype of their first customer. This is the customer that is going to be the first to adopt and purchase their product. The person who is ready and willing to purchase the product or service to address a need that is not being met. During this process, it is important to visualize the customer, give them a name and a visual appearance, address how they live, and even outline a day in the life of the customer.

One such project, from several years ago, was developed by a team of students who wanted to open an indoor softball arena. Their first customer was Joe Softball. He lived on the west side of Cincinnati near his four siblings and parents. He was thirty-four, worked five days a week as an engineer at GE aircraft engines, was married to his high school sweetheart, and had three pre-school children. He took a two-week vacation every year with his family and spent Sunday afternoons at either his parent's home or his in-law's home. One evening a week, and sometimes on the weekend, he liked to get together with his friends and play softball. Are you beginning to get the picture of Joe? Can you begin to better understand how Joe might use the arena? What kind of benefit Joe would be seeking from the experience? How much he might be willing to pay?

The fourth step is to evaluate and refine your product or service as needed to improve the experience for the customer. After their first visit to Lagos, Nigeria, the Tembo team we discussed earlier came back to their university classes with an idea about trying to combine cell phones and education. While in the US, the student team partnered with an educational program that had already been proven effective with their target student (children from infancy to age six), and they developed a prototype, i.e., a very basic version of the final concept. They then took that basic prototype back to Lagos. During this second trip, they worked with the local NGOs and cell phone service providers to get the product in the hands of their target audience and to learn more about the customer experience. This second trip was a vital step in the process of the development of this concept and resulted in several improvements to the product and company. In the end, while Tembo didn't win the final pitch competition, they competed very well, and the company is still making a difference in the world, by offering text-based educational products for children.[17]

LEAN STARTUP

The lean startup methodology, popularized by Eric Reis and Steve Blank,[18] provides one method for this process. This method for launching a new product came from the technology world but has application in many other products and services. The application of lean startup to this phase of analysis includes convincing prospective customers to use the product or service before developing a business plan with all the details for launching and building a new company. In order to accomplish this, the entrepreneur must develop a minimum viable product (MVP). Since getting them to buy the product is the ultimate test, the goal here is to convince users to not only *use* the product but also to *buy* the product.

While this may sound like a costly way to evaluate a business opportunity, there are often many creative ways to launch your product quickly and with a minimum of cost. One of my former students had an idea for ice cream for pets. In order to evaluate the product, she had to make sure dogs would enjoy the treat, of course, but she also had to learn more about whether customers would buy it. Taking it to the local farmers market was an inexpensive way to see if she could sell the product.

Just this week, a former student from Germany called to say hello and catch up. He was also calling to tell me about a new early-stage concept he is working on with two software designers. Earlier, when he was job hunting in Germany, he observed that the front desk experience at many companies was less than efficient and effective. This experience led him to reach out to people he knew who had software design experience and work with them to develop a basic version of a software concept to automate the front desk process in small- and medium-sized organizations. He had left his job at the beginning of the pandemic and decided to put his time and his own money into testing this process. The two designers are doing the same. The early results are good. In less than ten months, they have convinced ten companies to use the product. While they have suffered some lean times, they are now able to more confidently invest the money necessary to create a more extensive product.

With the lean method, the goal is not only to convince companies to buy the MVP but also to continually talk to those customers to learn more about their experience with the product. This information then provides a feedback loop to improve and iterate the concept. Bringing information on the customer experience back to your team, allows them to continually dig deeper and deeper into why the customer is having a particular experience. This kind of intense exploration can save tons of money and time and will ultimately answer the question of whether there is a viable market.

FINANCIAL VIABILITY

The third, but perhaps one of the most critical questions an entrepreneur must ask about a prospective opportunity is whether there is a financial reason to pursue this concept. It might seem obvious, but this step is one of the most avoided processes in the analysis of a new opportunity. I believe the reason is that many entrepreneurs are often both ignorant and unrealistic when it comes to understanding and addressing the financial side of an entrepreneurial venture. While they are most often incredibly brilliant people, they may not have the language or the skills associated with the financial analysis of an entrepreneurial opportunity. And even those with the skill set required can be blinded by their own enthusiasm and the encouragement of prospective customers and other interested parties. This often means when evaluating an exciting opportunity that is demonstrating great possibility for addressing a market problem, founders may ignore the financial feasibility until they have lost significant sums of money.

My students have taught me another reason why the financial aspect of a startup is so hard to grasp. They often tell me they are not comfortable with providing concrete numbers for an abstract concept. However, developing projections about financials is just like predicting the reactions of a marketplace. The process of developing a basic financial model for an entrepreneurial opportunity involves doing research and outlining and codifying assumptions. Remember, a new business is like any scientific research project. By clarifying the assumptions of a project, the researcher (or entrepreneur) can test each one to move closer and closer to the truth. The same applies to the financial analysis of a new startup.

While there are many books you might consider reviewing for assistance, for the novice, the starting point for this process is with your own goals. What kind of business do you want to pursue? Do you want to build wealth for later? Are you hoping to start a company that will pay your bills now and perhaps be an asset to pass on to your children? All of these can help you better understand whether this concept is a good financial fit for you.

Once you have given some consideration to the financial reason you are considering this opportunity, the next step is to evaluate the financial benefits compared to the financial costs of a specific entrepreneurial opportunity. The first series of questions are cost related. They must be answered by doing research on the costs associated with producing or acquiring the actual product or service. The key questions to ask here relate to identifying what it will cost to produce the product or service you intend to sell and what it will cost you to start up the business. It is important to make certain you are realistic and consider all the costs associated with not only getting started but also with the production or acquisition of the product or service you will offer, including your time and potential loss of income if you are not employed by someone else. Remember to keep a list of all the assumptions you make, so you can constantly go back and evaluate and modify them as needed. This constant evaluation and modification will allow you to continually move closer and closer to reality.

The next set of questions and assumptions are the financial benefits, the revenue. These are associated with much of the market research you have been working on in the earlier stages of the entrepreneurial opportunity evaluation process. These assumptions address questions such as what will people pay for this product or service and how much will it cost to acquire a customer? One additional, and very valuable, question to address is the lifetime value of a specific customer, also known as the lifetime customer value (LCV). In other words, from a financial perspective, what is each customer worth to the company? How often will they buy from you? Will this be a onetime purchase or will they be returning for replacement? Back to your assumptions, if it takes $500 to sell a customer $1,000 worth of product or services over the time period they are buying from you, then their contribution of LCV is $500. This is important because it helps you better understand where to put your time with respect to various customer groups. It also helps you understand how hard you must work for a specific financial goal.

After considering your personal financial goals, the costs and the benefits, or revenue that you could derive from the business, a simple mathematical formula can be used to determine whether the financial benefits to pursue this opportunity outweigh the costs. These six or seven simple questions are just a starting point for a better understanding of the financial aspect of an entrepreneurial opportunity. They do not address a full financial overview of your business. But they do provide an excellent litmus test for an entrepreneurial opportunity.

UNDERLYING REQUIREMENT: INTELLECTUAL HONESTY

Over the course of my career in entrepreneurship and in education, I have been blessed to know a few very special people, who were not only pioneers in entrepreneurship education but were also willing to share their time and wisdom with me personally to help advance my work. These people taught me no accomplishment in life is achieved with solitary effort and that we can all benefit greatly from being open to the wise counsel of others. I am frequently reminded of their influence in my life and work, and in the lives of those I am fortunate enough to touch as an educator.

Jeffry Timmons, mentioned earlier in this chapter, was one such person. Professor Timmons received his doctorate from Harvard and is probably best known for his work at Babson College, where he launched numerous innovative programs and helped Babson become one of the leading entrepreneurship schools in the world. Recently, I was reminded of Professor Timmons when I read an editorial in the *Wall Street Journal* about intellectual honesty. The author of the article was remembering the life of a famous scholar and commenting on her willingness to put intellectual honesty first in her scholarship. In his essay, he argued that intellectual honesty is an important yet often absent trait in much of today's research, which he argued is more likely to focus on simply trying to support the popular narrative of the day. Like the author of the editorial, Professor Timmons regarded intellectual honesty as a key trait necessary for success as an entrepreneur.

What is intellectual honesty, and why does it matter for entrepreneurs? Intellectual honesty might be defined simply as a focus on seeking the truth, even when it doesn't agree with your own personal beliefs. It means not lying to oneself, not pretending to know the truth when you don't; it means not omitting relevant facts purposely, and it means giving credit to sources of information where possible. For Professor Timmons, intellectual honestly was one of the key components in a coachable entrepreneur. And a coachable entrepreneur, he argued, is more likely to succeed and, therefore, present a good opportunity, for an investor and for a successful business. His guidelines suggested an entrepreneur who knows what they don't know is better prepared for the entrepreneurial journey than one who doesn't know what they don't know. Staying intellectually honest can be challenging. But for an entrepreneur, I agree with Professor Timmons' belief that it is a primary requirement for success.

The evaluation process is a critical step in the creative problem-solving process, and one that often causes a significant challenge for any creator. If we don't engage in seeking input on novel ideas, the ideas may never come to fruition. However, not only does this often feel risky as we may fear that our creation will be stolen or criticized, too much feedback can be confusing and exhausting. In the end, the savvy creator understands that there needs to be a plan for this evaluation phase and as the creator, it is important to not only stay open to input but also be discriminating in the application of feedback received. The key is to seek evaluation from the *right* people, legitimate experts in the field and prospective customers, and then after listening and considering the input, to trust your own instincts. Like every other aspect of entrepreneurship, learning to seek and utilize feedback is a skill that can be learned and improved upon with experience.

PRACTICE: CREATING VALUE

SEE

Ideas are not opportunities. Quantity of ideas is necessary for generating viable opportunities, but it is not sufficient. Remember there are four criteria for viable opportunities: interesting and worthwhile, timely, financially viable, and capable of creating value. Thus far, your practice has likely provided you with the information that can help you clarify whether a concept is interesting to you and worth pursuing and whether the time is right. But you are probably still unsure about the last two questions. Will any of the ideas I have generated be financially worthwhile and do any of them create real value? It is time to put your ideas to the test.

DO

Refine your ideas and select the top one to two you want to evaluate. Create a one-page overview of your concept. For each prospective opportunity, take everything you have learned and distill it into one page. This can be challenging because you want to include the most relevant data and information on why you believe this is a viable opportunity without getting too far into the weeds on the details. You will also want to have a prototype of your concept if possible. This may be a very basic version of your product or a diagram or description of your service or concept process. Make sure you include an archetype of your anticipated customers. Then, take the next step in evaluating your concept by talking to experts. These can be entrepreneurs, your mentor, someone who works or has worked in the industry related to your concept, or someone else you may know that you can trust to objectively evaluate your idea. Dig into the financial side if possible. Talk to someone who can help you understand whether this concept has the potential to generate money. Get as much feedback as you can. Listen and consider the input and make changes to your concept where needed. Remember, you may not want to make all the changes recommended.

REPEAT

After gathering input from experts, select the opportunity you believe has the greatest potential and consider how you can get feedback from prospective customers. The lean startup or design methods described in this chapter can help you create a way to gather information. Spend time getting to know your customer intimately and find a way to get meaningful feedback from them. To deeply understand your customer base, you will want to have a working prototype and perhaps even your first iteration of your product or service—what we call a minimum viable product. This will take time and effort, but you can practice this on a small scale also. For example, if you make fantastic cookies and think they can present a viable business opportunity, can you package up some and take them to a local farmers market? Or if you want to start a business helping people organize their homes and closets, can you put flyers advertising your service on the doors of neighbors and even offer your services to friends and family to get practice and feedback? If you are not yet sure which entrepreneurial opportunity will be yours, you don't have to wait. Try out the process. See what happens. It is a process that is open to anyone who decides to take on the practice of entrepreneurship. In the end, many of these evaluation steps are simply expanded versions of the classic lemonade stand! Make it a practice to thoroughly evaluate your opportunities with this model.

PART II
DOING

CHAPTER 4
TAKING ACTION

*Each time we face our fear, we gain strength,
courage, and confidence in the doing.*

—Theodore Roosevelt

Recognizing viable opportunities is required for entrepreneurship, but it is not sufficient. The next step of the See, Do, Repeat process, taking action, is often where the new entrepreneur begins to feel the full reality of the venture either emerge in full force or dissipate. This is the point where increased investments of time and money are required. The *doing* is the stage where we become committed and step into the big unknown. The decision to pursue your entrepreneurial dreams, full force, all in, will likely be the time when you make great sacrifices for your vision. You may leave your current job or decide to forego spending time with friends or family, in order to realize your entrepreneurial dreams. This is the proverbial fork in the road where some stop and others keep going. Are you ready? How many of the following are true for you?

- I believe I will succeed in reaching my entrepreneurial vision.
- I am able to achieve most goals that I set for myself.
- I am able to complete difficult tasks.
- I find my opportunity deeply interesting.
- I think about my new venture constantly.
- I am deeply committed to my new venture.

If you were able to say each of the above is true for you, then you are well on your way. If not, no worries. Regardless of your answers, there are several ways to help you feel more confident in taking the next steps on your entrepreneurial journey.

ENTREPRENEURIAL SELF-EFFICACY

There are countless stories of people who have dreamed big ideas, even discovered or created feasible business opportunities, but never took the step to bring their dream to fruition. Like opportunities, the willingness to evaluate the risks and take action will be heavily influenced by who are you are, what you know, and who you know. However, while there is no entrepreneurship without opportunities, it is the willingness to act on them that ultimately leads to a successful entrepreneurial venture. This is the second phase of the See, Do, Repeat practice.

DO

Moving from intention to action requires a belief that we can do what it takes to reach our entrepreneurial vision.

REPEAT

SEE

The willingness to take the action to start a new business begins with an intention. The reasons to start a business are many and can range from very personal and unique experiences to events or elements external to us that encourage us to consider turning an opportunity into a business. However, moving from intention to action requires a belief that we can do what it takes to reach our entrepreneurial vision. Psychologists often refer to the belief that we have the capacity to reach our goals as self-efficacy. Research has shown higher levels of self-efficacy mean we are more likely to focus on success, whereas lower levels mean we tend to focus more on feelings of failure. Higher self-efficacy also means we are better able to cope with adverse situations.[19] Having this kind of confidence in our abilities is what not only leads to the first steps into starting a business but will also carry you through the challenges, failures, and setbacks that are inevitably on the pathway to success.

Having this confidence in your ability to execute your goals is valuable in all aspects of life. In entrepreneurship, it is vital, not only to the success of the business but also to the health and well-being of any entrepreneur. As someone who has worked with hundreds of business founders, helping nascent entrepreneurs build this confidence has become a top priority. Psychologists have identified four ways to enhance self-efficacy which can be applied to the practice of entrepreneurship: mastery experiences, role models, coaching and mentoring, and a positive outlook.[20]

MASTERY EXPERIENCES

Mastery of any subject includes not only gaining knowledge but also applying it in multiple settings, with both positive and negative outcomes. Positive outcomes, or what we commonly think of as successes, tend to build confidence and therefore increase self-efficacy. Negative outcomes, or what we think of as failures, may initially undermine confidence. However, in the long run, addressing and learning from negative outcomes builds a more resilient self-efficacy that is even more powerful, and provides the ability to persevere in the face of adversity and to quickly rebound. By sticking it out through tough times, we emerge stronger from adversity. Therefore, investors are often more eager to invest in someone who has started a company, whether the company was a success or not, than in someone who has no experience with entrepreneurship.

Entrepreneurship, like any other set of skills, can be learned and practiced and, over time, can be enhanced. Education and experience in entrepreneurship are powerful tools to enhance confidence in your ability to take action.

Darren Berkovitz is the co-founder of TeleSign, a digital identity and programmable communications company, whose services are used by most of us on a regular basis. In 2005, after graduating from the University of Southern California, and two years before the iPhone was introduced, he and his business partners, Ryan Disraeli and Stacy Stubblefield, designed a system we all use and take for granted today. When a website needs to confirm your identity, they simply send you a text or call with a pin code you must enter for access to the website. At the time Telesign was founded, this two-factor authentication process didn't exist, and internet fraud was not yet the crisis it is today. Darren and his partners had identified a significant business opportunity. However, they may never have taken this step had they not experienced a high-quality experiential education and then joined a technology incubator, Curious Minds, which provided them with support and mastery experiences they needed to launch Telesign.

Returning to school and/or participating in programs designed to provide mastery experiences are both excellent ways to build your confidence to take the first step into a startup. However, there are many other ways to gain mastery experiences. They can range from working in a startup, to launching a new program or project at work, school, church, or other groups to which you belong. Either

DO

REPEAT

SEE

Entrepreneurship, like any other set of skills, can be learned and practiced and, over time, can be enhanced.

way you approach it, gaining mastery experiences is one of the best ways to build a strong sense of confidence in your ability to start and build an entrepreneurial venture. However, there are other valuable ways you can enhance your readiness for entrepreneurship and build your entrepreneurial self-efficacy.

ROLE MODELS AND CULTURE

For some there is never a question about whether they will be business owners. Sumita Batra is a celebrity stylist, entrepreneur, and CEO of Ziba Beauty. Sumita's curiosity and passion for authentic eastern beauty traditions, introduced the Art of Threading™ to the US over thirty years ago. She is the author of *The Art of Mehndi*, which showcases her work with celebrity clients like Beyoncé, Madonna, Gwen Stefani, and Christina Aguilera and details her mehndi methodology and technique. Her work has graced the pages of *Vanity Fair, Rolling Stone, Mademoiselle,* and *The New York Times Magazine.*

With over thirty years of experience as an entrepreneur and pioneer in the beauty industry, Sumita has an amazing story of hard work, failure, and success as an entrepreneur. Sumita spent her formative years in India, after her family fled Iran for religious and political reasons. During their time in India, her mother developed a passion for the beauty industry and obtained her beauty license there. When the family later relocated to LA, she took a job and soon converted her Indian beauty license into a US esthetics license. After losing her job, Sumita's mother started Ziba Beauty (*Ziba* means "beautiful" in Persian). At just eighteen years of age, Sumita joined the business. The family (most of whom also work in the company) quickly realized she was a born business leader, and soon she became the CEO. When I asked about her decision to be an entrepreneur, she simply replied, ". . . this is what you do."

Like Sumita, many of my students are born into families and cultures where entrepreneurship is the norm and often expected. They have entrepreneurial role models from a very young age. But for many others, entrepreneurship is not considered an option.

For example, one of my recent graduate students, who was born to Indian parents, is pursuing entrepreneurship despite his family role models and values. According to this young man, his parents provided him with only a few options for his life's work. They expected him to be a physician or an engineer, and if he couldn't succeed in either of those professions, a lawyer. For his parents, success was having a stable and secure position in a profession. He studied computer science (because it was close to engineering and would satisfy his father), but his work experiences to date have not met his passion. So, he is now returning to school, midcareer, to study entrepreneurship. And his story is not a unique one. Many people find they can pursue their passion for entrepreneurship only after they have tested other options. While business startups always require stepping into the unknown and taking risks, for these founders, the decision to take the path of entrepreneurship can often require an extra dose of bravery and courage, as they take the road not traveled by their role models.

Having a parental role model who has been or is an entrepreneur has been shown to increase one's belief in their ability to succeed as a business owner. However, even though research has demonstrated having an entrepreneurial family member or close relative will increase the likelihood a person will also pursue business ownership, the importance of role models in building self-efficacy can be extended to others who were not born into these families. Our preferences to engage behaviors are constantly influenced by the ideas and behaviors of others and by the stories about their lives and experiences they share. Regardless of whether you have entrepreneurial role models in your family, if you want to increase your confidence in your ability to succeed as an entrepreneur, one way to do so is to surround yourself with successful entrepreneurs and to learn by listening to their stories of both success and failure. This is exactly why I started the *EnFactor Podcast*, to share stories that will inspire and motivate aspiring entrepreneurs. But listening to their stories is not the only way to build confidence in your ability to reach your entrepreneurial dreams. Another very valuable aspect of building entrepreneurial self-efficacy is by finding a coach or mentor.

COACHING AND MENTORING

There is no doubt pursuing a new business venture takes a substantial dose of courage and bravery. We often think of entrepreneurs as a unique group of people who are more willing to take risks than the general population. From the outside looking in, entrepreneurs do often appear to be taking big risks. And, of course, there are many who take extreme risks. But, in reality, the majority of successful entrepreneurs do not have a significantly different risk profile from non-entrepreneurs. Some are risk averse, and others are more likely to seek out risks. However, there is a commonality among successful entrepreneurs. They are willing to identify and consider as many of those risks as possible in advance. And by acknowledging and evaluating them, they attempt to determine those aspects of their plan that are most vulnerable to failure. They can then decide whether, when, and how to take action. In other words, successful entrepreneurs take *calculated* risks.

For Brad Chisum, it was one of his university professors who gave him the confidence to make the move from corporate to startup. Brad is the co-founder of Launch Factory, a startup studio in San Diego. This program, like many others, is designed to help launch new business ventures. He decided to start this company because of what he learned on his own entrepreneurial journey as the co-founder of Lumedyne Technologies, a MEMS Inertial Sensor company. MEMS Inertial Sensors are the technology that makes accelerators and gyroscopes which, at the time of the Lumedyne launch, was relatively new but are now found everywhere, including in your cell phone.

When I talked with Brad, he confessed he initially didn't think he could be an entrepreneur because he "knew nothing about business." He was an engineer and had a great

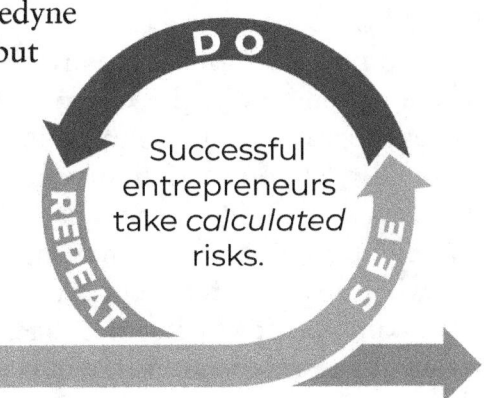

Successful entrepreneurs take *calculated* risks.

job but realized he was actually a "closet entrepreneur." So, he decided to go back to school. Brad credits one of his professors during his MBA program with teaching him what Brad calls the real story about entrepreneurship. It included two important facts about entrepreneurship that enabled him to move forward and leave his job and start Lumedyne. According to Brad, the first is that no individual person has what it takes to willpower a business to success, because so much is out of your control. You cannot control markets, you cannot control your competition, you even cannot control who works for you. You can influence some factors, but in the end, by yourself, you can't get it done. Second, there will be people who come along and help you on your journey; the key is to be open to this help and be willing to accept it.

For Brad, knowing that no single person can succeed as an entrepreneur alone but that there would be help along the way, meant there was hope for him. In the end, knowing he didn't have to do this alone was reassuring and gave him the courage to take what he calls a "leap of faith" and start Lumedyne, which was sold to Google in 2015 for a reported eighty-five million dollars.

By returning to graduate school, Brad opened his network to include people who could coach and mentor him on his entrepreneurial journey. However, you don't have to invest in an advanced degree to find a coach or mentor. There are many formal programs that have a mission of connecting entrepreneurs with people who have the experience and expertise to provide powerful coaching and mentoring. SCORE (Service Corp of Retired Executives) and the SBA (Small Business Administration) are two programs that have provided free coaching for millions of entrepreneurs in the US for decades. And there are many newer programs available today in virtually every community and online. (In Chapter 6, I discuss more of these programs and how to access them.) However, while there is not a shortage of coaches and mentors, one of the challenges many entrepreneurs face is knowing how to effectively engage with this valuable resource.

Taking full advantage of a coaching or mentoring relationship requires the intellectual honesty we discussed in the previous chapter. But what does that mean in a practical sense? First, it means developing strong listening skills. For an enthusiastic and passionate entrepreneur, this means being open to hearing something different from what you thought we knew. It can also mean to stop talking and trying to impress the listener with what you already know long enough to learn from them. I often think of this as having the ability to adopt what is referred to as *Shoshin*, or a "beginner's mind," in Zen Buddhism. A story I heard many years ago illustrates this concept.

Once, there was a wise Zen master. People would come from far and near to seek his counsel and to ask for wisdom. One day a student visited the Zen master and asked for enlightenment. The student was so excited to be there, and he wanted to impress the famous master, so he proceeded to tell the master many things he had learned and practiced. Soon the master interrupted him to suggest they have tea. The student really didn't want to take the time for tea, but the Zen master seemed insistent, so the student acquiesced and sat down to have tea. As the tea brewed, the student began to talk again. The Zen master was silent. When the tea was ready, the Zen master began to pour. As he poured the tea, the student continued to talk, and the Zen master continued to pour. The student talked and talked, and the master poured and poured until the tea began to spill over the cup. As the tea continued to run down the side of the cup and onto the floor, the student stopped talking and then cried out, "Enough! You are spilling the tea. Can't you see the cup is full?" In response, the master stopped pouring and smiled at his guest. He then said, "You are like this teacup, so full of what you already know, nothing more can be added. If you seek enlightenment, come back to me with an empty mind."

Being open doesn't mean we blindly take all the advice we get. In fact, one of the questions I get from students most is about what to do when they get conflicting advice from those coaches. In this case, it is helpful to remember that business decision-making, which includes launching a new business venture, is simply based on a series of hypotheses and experiments. The goal then becomes to remain not only humble and open, but doing so with a critical and intellectually honest mind. In other words, the perspective of the basic research guidelines, of testing and constantly questioning findings, will guide you as you assess and evaluate what you have learned from your coaching and mentoring relationships.

While everything you learn can have a purpose, you are ultimately the decision-maker in your entrepreneurial journey. The ability to remain open to constantly stress testing each hypothesis is critical to maintaining this state of intellectual honesty as an entrepreneur. However, this must be followed by an honest and reflective assessment of the data and findings.

To take full advantage of a coaching relationship, stop doing all the talking and make room for something new; even if you ultimately decide not to take the advice of the mentor, you will be changed by being open and approaching your business goals with a beginner's mind. Building your skills as a coachable entrepreneur will allow you to find and take advantage of trusted mentors who can help you build your entrepreneurial self-efficacy.

While mastery experiences, role models, and effective coaching experiences can go a long way toward building entrepreneurial self-efficacy, intention and action are also governed by your own expectations of outcomes. It is also important to learn to manage your own beliefs. With respect to building self-efficacy, a positive outlook can be the key to a willingness to take entrepreneurial action.

POSITIVE OUTLOOK ON THE FUTURE

A positive outlook can be the key to a willingness to take entrepreneurial action.

Numerous research studies have identified a relationship between entrepreneurship and holding a positive outlook regarding the future. One interesting study,[21] based on data from 5,000 households (12,000 individuals) in the UK, looked at whether people who became entrepreneurs were more positive about the financial results of starting their own business than those who did not start a business. In this study, the researchers examined data that had been reported over an eighteen-year period to see if those individuals who had higher expectations about the financial rewards of leaving their current employment and starting a business were more likely to do so. What they found was not only were those who were more positive about the rewards of self-employment more likely to pursue a startup, they found that those positive feelings actually increased once they became self-employed.

A positive outlook is defined a number of ways, but most simply it is often thought of as one end of a continuum of attitude toward experiences and outcomes. It is viewed as a contrast to expectations that the future will be bad or scary. Once thought of as an enduring personality trait, many psychologists have had success with helping people move from a consistently negative view of experiences to a more positive one.

Improving your perspective on the future does not mean that you become delusional. Those with a more positive outlook simply do not ruminate, since the almost endless loop of rumination tends to block action. It is no surprise that those with a more positive outlook spend less time in worry and more time taking action to create the future they envision.

Have you ever kept a diary of your worries and then looked back at them? I tried this one time. It was literally life changing for me to see that 100% of my worries never materialized. During that time there were problems and negative outcomes for sure, but the big worries I had never happened. Worry and pessimism just get in the way of our willingness to take action. Sometimes we must feel the fear and do it anyway.

Our perspective on the future can change throughout our life. There may be times in our life when we are able to look forward with a positive and confident perspective. Then there are times when we are feeling drained from change and loss. That is when it can be the hardest to hold on to a positive view of the future. But that is exactly the time when we need to dig deep, to find the power within us to take action. Life is telling us that it is time for a change. And change requires action.

I recall reading a book many years ago entitled *Feel the Fear and Do It Anyway* by Dr. Susan Jeffers. This was a time in my life when I was a single mom of two very young children and working on a PhD. Her book was a gift to me at a time when everything was feeling pretty scary. Decision-making was especially hard for me at the time. As a single parent, I missed having someone to talk to about even the small day-to-day decisions with my children. And, in other areas of my life, there was a lot of uncertainty. What would I do when I soon completed my PhD? Where would I work and live? Jeffers' book helped me develop a model for decision-making that I have used throughout the rest of my life.

In her book, Jeffers draws from Stewart Emery's book *Actualizations*, where he shares his model for changing your perspective. He developed this model while he was on the flight deck of an airplane on the way to Hawaii, where he noticed a console and inquired about its purpose. The pilot informed Emery that this was an inertial guidance system for the airplane. The purpose of the system, he further explained, was to get the plane to its destination within five minutes of the planned arrival time. The system worked by correcting the path of the aircraft each time it went off course. Furthermore, the pilot explained, although they would arrive as planned, the plane would only be on the actual course about 10% of the time! As Emery considered this fact, he realized that life is the same. The path to where we want to go starts with an error, which we then correct toward another error, which we then correct to the next error, and so on. The only time we are truly on course is that

> **DO**
> **REPEAT**
> **SEE**
> The trick to life is not to worry about making a wrong decision, it's learning when to correct

moment when we zigzag across the path. Jeffers and Emery taught me that "[t]he trick to life is not to worry about making a wrong decision, it's learning when to correct."

Adopting this notion of decision-making came as a tremendous relief to me at a time when so much was changing in my life. For me, this meant I could embrace the decisions that were facing me with a lighter, less restrictive approach. It meant I could enjoy my life more because I wasn't so afraid that any one decision I made would mean I had done irreparable damage to my children's lives or my own life. It reminded me that I could make mistakes and still survive. I could let go and surrender a bit more to life and the bounty being offered to me. It meant I could face the future with a more positive attitude. It also meant I could confidently take action.

I have encountered many optimistic entrepreneurs throughout my career. One that stands out is Danny Mastranardo. Danny and his brothers started Nardo's Naturals, a natural skin care company that was featured on ABC's *Shark Tank*. The pathway to their success has not been easy. In fact, they faced extreme tragedy when one of the brothers died unexpectantly in a car crash. However, when Danny tells the story of their success, from leaving behind his dream job to crashing at their parent's condo and mixing up skin care in his mom's kitchen to becoming a leading manufacturer of organic skin care products, Danny stays positive and focused on the joy of working with his brothers to build this dream company. He also tells stories of how he and his brothers have been willing to take action, even when they were scared and felt totally overwhelmed with inexperience and uncertainty. This is the kind of

DO
REPEAT
SEE

Your own entrepreneurial journey also requires the willingness to take action.

outlook on the future that is required to not only start a business but also the kind that is required to sustain it.

Your own entrepreneurial journey also requires the willingness to take action. This requires intention, courage, and confidence in your ability to figure it out along the way. Building mastery skills, with the help of role models and coaches and mentors, and through your own tenacity and positive outlook, you can move beyond seeing opportunities to actually bringing your vision to life. In the next two chapters, we will look more closely at some of the skills you need to master and the people and organizations you need to know to help you take the next steps required on your own entrepreneurial journey.

PRACTICE: BUILDING ENTREPRENEURIAL SELF-EFFICACY

SEE

We always learn something from taking action; sometimes we learn what to do, sometimes we learn what not to do. Entrepreneurship is always an experiment. Because we are trying to impact the future with our actions today, we are never completely certain of outcomes. Just like all learning, over time we come to know cause and effect, and we can make informed decisions about our action. This is the essence of building your self-efficacy, building confidence in your ability to generate positive outcomes. If you completed the previous practice exercises, you have already demonstrated your willingness to take action by building in rituals and seeking input on your concepts. However, if you read them and decided to wait to take any real action on them, you may want to ask yourself why. Is it that you are not ready? Are you waiting until a time in the future when you are better prepared? Or is it that you think you are not the entrepreneurial type? Are you afraid your idea isn't any good or that it will be a waste of your time, effort, and money? Is your plan to do something someday but not now? If you haven't taken any action yet, reflect on why and consider what might be holding you back from pursuing your entrepreneurial dreams. Remember, the simple act of reading this book is a start and it is telling you something.

DO

Consider incorporating the methods for building your self-confidence and your entrepreneurial self-efficacy. The entire focus of this book is on helping you practice the skills you need to succeed as an entrepreneur. If you didn't take action in the previous chapter exercises, go back and do so now. If you did take the steps, were there areas you skipped or ignored? If so, go back and complete them now. If you feel confident in your effort on earlier exercises, consider how you can enhance your entrepreneurial self-efficacy through a mastery experience, role models, coaching, and a positive outlook. Pick one of the methods and take action on it. For example, attend a class or program in your community to gain mastery skills in some area of entrepreneurship, or reach out to your local SCORE chapter and find a coach. You can even listen to a podcast and learn more about how others have succeeded. Take one step toward building up your entrepreneurial self-efficacy.

REPEAT

Building your entrepreneurial self-efficacy takes time and effort. Successful entrepreneurs build self-efficacy by doing. Even if you are not yet running your own company, you can begin to build your confidence. To do so requires practice and that means incorporating the techniques that build self-efficacy into your life. Set aside some time each week to work on one or more of the four ways outlined in this chapter. For each one there are options that are simple, easy, and often free, and there are more intense experiences that require a greater investment of time and/or money. Create your own customized program to enhance your self-efficacy with some of the ideas below:

- *Mastery* experiences—can range from watching programs on TV to signing up for a class, joining an incubator, or seeking a university degree.

- Engaging with *role models*—can be as simple as listening to the *EnFactor Podcast* or similar programs, attending a speaker event, or meeting with successful entrepreneurs.

- Taking advantage of *coaching*—can be as simple as reaching out to your local SCORE chapter or asking a neighbor or teacher to be your coach, to hiring a professional coach.

- Learning to have a more *positive outlook* on the future— can be as simple as keeping a journal and becoming more self-aware, to seeking out professional help to examine and perhaps even reframe your perspective.

CHAPTER 5

YOUR ENTREPRENEURSHIP EDUCATION

Education is not preparation of life. Education is life itself.

—John Dewey

The pursuit of an opportunity is a learning process. Perhaps more than any other skill, entrepreneurs become good at learning. Every new venture is an experiment. Much like the famous line from the movie *Field of Dreams*, each entrepreneur steps into the unknown believing that "if I build it, they will come." Otherwise, why would anyone ever take the risk? Of course, there is a lot of work that has gone into understanding why this may be true. But, even so, having confidence in our opportunity and ourselves is what gets us to the starting line. When we take the step across and start the marathon, we are going to need to be ready to be constantly learning. What kind of learner are you? Are you ready to learn?

- I enjoy learning.
- When faced with a question or task I don't understand, I quickly seek out help.
- I frequently create opportunities to learn something new.
- I view most experiences as an opportunity to learn.
- I routinely learn from the experiences and guidance of others.
- I understand how I learn best.

LEARNING AND ENTREPRENEURSHIP

Most entrepreneurs become highly proficient at self-education. I recently had the chance to talk with Sean Green and Eric Heiert, the co-founders of Safehouse in Austin, Texas. These young men were high school classmates and friends of my son and daughter, so I have known them for many years.

Today Sean has ten years of experience creating content and developing brands on the internet that he has perfected through his previous positions as the creative director at Twitch and a visual storyteller at Esports. Eric is a livestream event producer who has produced hundreds of digital events as a talent buyer, media coordinator, and program director.

Together Sean and Eric have created a livestream production that showcases interactive music performances online. It is their mission to empower musicians through a modern approach to discoverability and autonomy in the music industry, through livestreaming. Since their launch five years ago, Safehouse has hosted over 200 shows, featuring over 800 artists, for nearly one million music lovers from all corners of the world.

Despite some early success, Eric and Sean are facing some real challenges. As I write this, we have been amid an international pandemic for about a year. Not surprisingly, this uncontrollable environmental variable has opened a significant opportunity for them. Their business suddenly became more viable, as the entire world's willingness and skills associated with using technology advanced what might have taken twelve years in a single year. As leaders in this concept, they have been struggling for the past five years to build the company. But now they must move quickly to take advantage of the opportunities presented. Neither of them has a background in entrepreneurship, but like many entrepreneurs, they bring a passion and a lot of hard work to their early-stage company.

As I talked to them, it was amazing how much they had learned in the past five years, and I am very proud of them. However, it was clear they needed help. Fortunately for them and their company, they are humble and anxious for coaching, guidance, and connections, because they have realized how much they don't know. Chinese philosopher Lau Tsu is credited with the famous saying, "When the student is ready, the teacher will appear." Now that the students are ready, the teachers are beginning to appear. The same will be true for you as you take the first steps on your own entrepreneurial journey.

The quote for the opening of this chapter is taken from the writing of John Dewey, a famous educational philosopher, who believed educational programs should be representative of a social environment and that students learn best when in natural social settings. Based on his philosophy, many educational programs have adopted what is often referred to as experiential education. This is not new. Most of us are very familiar with this concept in fields such as medicine. After they complete medical school, a new MD works for a period in a hospital or medical environment under the tutelage of other practicing physicians. However, in more recent years, the idea of the practice of one's training as a student has become more prevalent in many other fields. This is true in entrepreneurship education, where most programs now have some experiential components to their program.

There has been significant debate over the years regarding whether entrepreneurship can be taught. Several years ago, I invited my friend and colleague Dr. Steve Spinelli into my graduate class as a guest speaker. Steve is a co-founder of Jiffy Lube International and is currently the president of Babson College, a leader and one of the top-ranked institutions for entrepreneurship education in higher education.

During my class, the topic of whether entrepreneurship is something that is in our DNA or whether it is something that can be taught and learned in an educational context was broached. Steve asked one of my students to name the busiest highway in the area. We were in the Cincinnati, Ohio, area, so my students said I-75. He then asked how many of them would be willing to try to cross the highway blindfolded if the prize for doing so successfully was one million dollars. Of course, there were very few takers despite the large sum (there was one young man who said he would try because it was a "parking lot" at that time). Nevertheless, most were not interested in taking on that challenge because of the high risk associated.

Steve then asked how many would try to cross the highway without the blindfold. More were willing to take the chance because the risk had been reduced. He then suggested that through entrepreneurship education, we can take off the blindfold and reduce some of the risk associated with a business startup. There still may be accidents or even tragedy if miscalculations are made, but hopefully, there are fewer. No one can give you the motivation, the drive, and the confidence to take the steps necessary to start a new venture, but through education, you can improve the odds and reduce the risk. Over the years, I have heard a similar sentiment from many entrepreneurs, who told my students how much they would've benefited from some of the lessons our students can learn through entrepreneurship education. And, interestingly, it is not just the lessons but also the context.

More recently, film producer, director, playwriter, and entrepreneur Jeffrey Madoff visited my class. Jeff is the founder of top-rated New York City video production company Madoff Productions and author of *Creative Careers: Making a Living with Your Ideas.* Jeff has edited and directed award-winning commercials, documentaries, and web content around the world for clients such as Ralph Lauren, Tiffany & Co, Radio City, The American Academy of Dramatic Arts, and Harvard University. One of my students asked him if he regretted not getting a degree in entrepreneurship before he became an entrepreneur. He said, that while he had no regrets about his pathway, what he would have gained from an entrepreneurship education was the network. Now, as an adjunct professor at the world-renowned Parsons Design School, he reminds his students that the network of peers and professionals they are afforded access to as students is like currency. The same is true for you. The network you build, as you build your entrepreneurial skills, will be invaluable to your efforts.

Your entrepreneurship education will start as soon as you take the first steps to explore a business concept. This education will happen regardless of what you do. But as Dr. Spinelli and Jeff both point out, a curated education may reduce your risk and be more efficient and valuable in the long run. However, gaining the knowledge you need to launch a business doesn't have to mean a college degree. Certainly, pursuing formal education is an option. And, fortunately for you, there are many options now available. Since I first entered the field many years ago, the number of schools offering a course and degree programs has grown exponentially. Besides college courses and degree programs, there are many other options available that range from certificate programs to coaching and mentoring programs to peer connection groups. In fact, there are so many options today, navigating them can be daunting. As you get started, you need to know what to learn as well as how to learn.

It is important to remember, that whether you use a personally designed self-study program or decide to pursue a certification or advance degree program, you will be learning. And, as Dewey points out, learning is not just preparation for your entrepreneurial journey, it is the journey. I can assure you, the pathway to a successful business will be a learning journey.

CUSTOMIZING YOUR LEARNING JOURNEY

Up to this point, this book has addressed the importance of recognizing and evaluating opportunities and embracing the intention and willingness to take action. Entrepreneurial self-efficacy is key to that willingness. And, as you now know, mastery experiences, role models, coaches and mentors, and a positive outlook can help you build self-efficacy. Embedded in this process is learning. In fact, as you learn, you will naturally become more confident in your ability to execute and realize your entrepreneurial vision. Developing a personalized educational pathway can be instrumental in this process.

Let's start with *how* to learn. Every learner is different, and only you can decide what works best for you. However, my instructional design efforts have been influenced by the work of several educators, who developed a model for situational cognition.[22] This model identifies five modes of learning which can be accessed to create a rich learning experience. These include collaboration, coaching/mentoring, reflection, apprenticeship, and multiple practice. While I have used this model in the design of formal educational programs, it also works in informal self-directed education.

One of the best examples, of the application of situated cognition in action, is the story of the friendship between two prolific inventors Thomas Edison and Henry Ford. Ford met his boyhood hero, Edison, in 1896 at a conference in New York. Soon thereafter, Edison invited Ford to visit his new winter home on the Caloosahatchee River in Fort Myers, Florida. Ford later purchased property and built a home next door to the Edisons. During their time in Florida, the two decided to take a camping trip to the Everglades. While they had to turn back from the initial trip because it became too rough, this trip spawned a series of camping and auto trips taken by the two great entrepreneurs.

Over the years, the friends added Henry Firestone (Firestone Tires) and John Burroughs (a naturalist and writer) to their annual camping and automobile treks around the eastern US. The four mixed pleasure and business, and out of those fireside conversations, hundreds of innovations emerged. While Edison began as a *mentor* to Ford, they *collaborated* to produce numerous commercialized inventions, spent long hours *reflecting* during their camping trips, became *apprentices* in a wide variety of fields and industries, and applied what they learned using *multiple practice* to find workable solutions.

COLLABORATION

Peer learning can be simply defined as students learning from other students. The types and methods associated with peer learning are vast—from formal to informal and from designed experiences to spontaneous ones. Regardless of the format, there is significant research to support the power of learning from others who are in a similar state of knowledge and experience with respect to a specific topic. Quite simply, reciprocal or peer learning works by providing learners a broader perspective and by providing meaningful connections. In other words, because each of us comes to a learning experience with different levels of prior knowledge, experiences, and networks as well as varying capacities to learn selected topics, collaborative learning will expand the scope of what each student can learn and experience.

There are numerous programs designed to provide aspiring and nascent entrepreneurs with collaborative experiences. In the next chapter, I will provide much more detail on both longer-term and short-term (think one evening or a weekend) co-working experiences that you can use to broaden your knowledge of entrepreneurship. However, as I mentioned earlier, not only do collaborative learning experiences provide you with more than you might learn solo, but they can also provide opportunities to connect with like-minded people and may even lead to long-term partnerships.

One example of this is the story of Miles and AJ, an LA-based videography and photography director duo. AJ (Andrew) Favicchio was a student of mine and a very talented videographer. After graduating from the University of Tampa, AJ started a freelance company producing videos and providing photography for weddings, corporate clients, and virtually anyone who could use his services. While he was working in Tampa, he collaborated with Miles Cable on some projects and the two decided to move to LA as a directing duo. Today, the pair has worked on both commercial and music-related projects for industry giants, such as Interscope, Hyatt, Columbia Records, and Disney, and has collaborated with some of the world's most popular artists, like Billie Eilish, Adam Lambert, and CNCO, on videos amassing hundreds of millions of views. Like Sean and Eric, Miles and AJ found they were complementary to each other and that together they could be so much more than working alone. Collaboration is not only a great way to learn from peers, but it may also be the pathway to your business.

COACHING AND MENTORING

In the previous chapter, working with a coach and/or a mentor was identified as an important way to build the entrepreneurial self-efficacy needed to execute on an opportunity. This process works because coaches and mentors are an excellent source of knowledge. They can not only serve as guides to help you learn important skills along the way, but they can also hold you accountable for your learning and provide you with an assessment of what you are learning.

REFLECTION

If you want to gain the most from your learning experiences, it is important to include reflection with your peer learning experiences and your work with a coach or mentor. These three combined are a powerful learning trifecta. While collaboration allows for peer learning and coaching and mentoring can bring you expert advice, reflection is where you can actually internalize and personalize what you are learning.

A few years ago, I read Cal Newton's book, *Deep Work: Rules for Focused Success in a Distracted World*. The premise of the book is that the ability to engage in deep work, which is something cognitively demanding, can be a "superpower" in our hyper-stimulating, full-of-interruptions world. Providing examples of how the greatest innovators utilized deeply cognitive and creative work to advance their purpose and change the world in his book, he provides tools and techniques for building more reflection and deep work into your daily life.

As a university professor for most of my life, I have been and am frequently engaged in creative work that requires deep thought and focus. I have always been good at getting lost in my work. My family might say I am *too* good. They know that when I am focused, they are not being heard and I am probably not aware of what is happening around me. But that is not the point. The point is, even though I am capable of deep focus, my day-to-day life typically doesn't provide me with enough opportunity to address the deep work I yearn to produce. If I want to focus on deep work, I must plan for it, and I have to build it into my life as a routine.

While there are many ways to build reflection time into your life, one of the easiest ways is to have a journal or notebook and set aside time each day to simply reflect and write. This type of learning is cognitively demanding and requires a discipline few other learning formats demand. AJ Favicchio, the student I discussed previously in this chapter, reminded me of a book and program I had used at an earlier time in my life. Understanding the role of reflection in his own learning journey, AJ found time for creative, cognitive work using a program outlined by Julia Cameron in her book, *The Artist's Way*. In this book, the author shares her own story of reflection using a daily writing ritual and outlines a program the reader can follow.

Growing up in a family floral business, I learned very quickly that when someone died in our small community, we had to all show up to work. No matter what I had planned with my friends, if the work required my help, I had to change my plans to help in our family business. Funeral flowers were critical to the bottom line. This is where the bulk of our profits resided. They were generally less expensive and typically required less time to assemble than flowers for a wedding, for example. So, we all worked in the business when customer demand required. This is true for many small business owners.

It was challenging for my mom to hire enough talented labor at the salary her small business could afford. So, she worked in the business constantly and brought in family as needed. She had little time to reflect on strategy or scenario planning. She was on the front lines, every day, keeping the doors of her business open. Many entrepreneurs must work this way and in so doing they miss out on the opportunity to work ON their business, because they are always working IN their business.

Today, this is perhaps even more true than it was when I was young. With the distraction of social media and the possibility and even expectation of being constantly connected, our lives provide precious little time for reflection. However, if you want to get the most from your learning journey as an entrepreneur, you will need to build a reflection routine into your life.

APPRENTICESHIP

Since the Middle Ages, trades and skills have been developed by working alongside a master in the field. Gaining the level of mastery, requires not only having knowledge and the ability to apply that knowledge in practice but also someone who can teach the skills necessary to succeed. While entrepreneurship doesn't require an apprenticeship in order to practice, the concept can still be quite valuable. Much like working with a coach, seeking out experiences that allow you to learn more about not only the practice of entrepreneurship but also the industry of interest can be extremely valuable.

For our students, we recommend finding successful entrepreneurs and asking to shadow them for a day or a week. We also encourage internships and even volunteering in entrepreneurial companies to learn more about what day-to-day operations entail. Any type of work experience, even a short-term or summer job, can be invaluable.

When my mother decided it was time for her to retire from her floral business, she asked me if I wanted to take over the operations. At the time I was in graduate school and did not want to return to the small rural town where the business was located. At that time in my life, taking over the family business didn't seem like the right path for me. However, one of my high school classmates had worked in the business from time to time and had learned as an apprentice from my mother, and for her, it was a logical next step to buy the business. An apprenticeship was an ideal way to learn about the business and business ownership prior to taking the next step.

MULTIPLE PRACTICE

Earlier I likened entrepreneurship to the practice of yoga. Like yoga, one never perfects entrepreneurship. It is a learning experience every day. Recognizing this is part of a healthy entrepreneurial mindset. An acceptance that learning is a fundamental part of the journey and you will be given the opportunity to refine and hone your entrepreneurial skills repeatedly along the way can be extremely empowering.

In our educational programs, we don't expect that the first concept a student pursues will necessarily succeed. It is quite common for successful entrepreneurs to have had a few failures along the way to success. A few years ago, I was at a biotech conference listening to a panel of investors who focus on medical and biotechnology opportunities. One of the investors was talking about the profile of the ideal entrepreneur. Like most investors, he had indicated that he is investing in people, not just ideas or concepts. When he described the ideal candidate for his investments, he said he prefers someone who has experienced entrepreneurship, even if their earlier attempts had been failures. Why? Because of the learning experience that comes with the practice of entrepreneurship.

Think about this idea with respect to selling, pitching, or negotiating skills that every entrepreneur needs to possess. These are skills that require practice, preferably in the field. We don't learn any of these skills by just doing them once. They require practice and making mistakes and correcting those in order to gain mastery. Learning about entrepreneurship requires showing up every day, keeping a beginner's mind, learning from everything and everyone, and trying not to ever repeat the same mistakes.

COMPONENTS OF AN ENTREPRENEURSHIP EDUCATION

It is beyond the scope of this book to cover everything you will need to know as an entrepreneur. In fact, no one can know in advance everything you will need to know. You will have your own learning journey. But after years of the practice of entrepreneurship and as an educator in the field, I can share some basics that will help you and remove the blindfold referenced by Dr. Spinelli. The following list of topics may be helpful if you decide to build your own customized education.

BASIC BUSINESS SKILLS

First and foremost, a basic understanding of accounting is vital to your education. Accounting is often referred to as the language of business. You need to get comfortable with numbers and with basic financial statements. You don't want to leave all of this to your accountant. Besides accounting, understanding and reducing risk is extremely important. And, again, you want to know the questions to ask your attorney and how to find a good attorney. Keep in mind that lawyers, like accountants, specialize, so you will want to make sure they have experience in the issue you need them to address. Otherwise, you will be paying for their time to become educated to help you.

Beyond these two areas, there are a number of others in business and entrepreneurship, you should build into your educational program. The list below is not comprehensive, but it provides a good place to start.

1. Accounting: the language of business, basics you need to know
    - Terminology
    - Margin

- Cash flow
- Understanding the financial levers that drive your business
- How to read basic financial statements
- Funding your venture
- How to find the right accountant

2. Risk Mitigation and Regulation: knowing how to protect yourself and your assets
    - Legal entity formation
    - Intellectual property protection
    - Contracts
    - Insurance
    - Licensing and permits
    - How to find the right attorney

3. Business Models and Strategy: how to plan and share that plan
    - Key components of a business plan
    - Business model canvas
    - How to conduct business research
    - How to build an operational plan
    - How to communicate and pitch your vision and strategy

4. Marketing: knowing how to identify and communicate with your audience
    - Defining a market
    - Accessing a market
    - Reaching a market
    - Messaging
    - Metrics

5. People: knowing how to build a team
   - Load the bus first philosophy
   - Understanding key components of a team
   - Creating a shared vision[23]
   - Understanding how to manage and lead

ENTREPRENEURIAL MINDSET

Beyond basic business skills, the development of an entrepreneurial mindset can be a goal, as you build your entrepreneurial know-how. One of the tools I use to help my students gain a better understanding of their own entrepreneurial mindset is the Entrepreneurial Mindset Profile (EMP)® assessment.[24] Based on extensive research, the designers identified fourteen scales where entrepreneurs scored significantly different from corporate managers. Among those scales, they identified seven that were skills-based. Based on their research, self-reported entrepreneurs scored higher than corporate managers in six of those skills: *a focus on the future, the ability to generate ideas, execution, self-confidence, optimism,* and *persistence.*

In the end, entrepreneurship is a practice, and no matter what you study or how you prepare, you will never know everything you need to know before you get started. However, the important thing to know is it will be a learning process first and foremost. Keeping an open mind and intellectual honesty is vital. The process of building a company is transformative for any entrepreneur. You will learn far more than you can imagine. Some lessons will be very hard, some

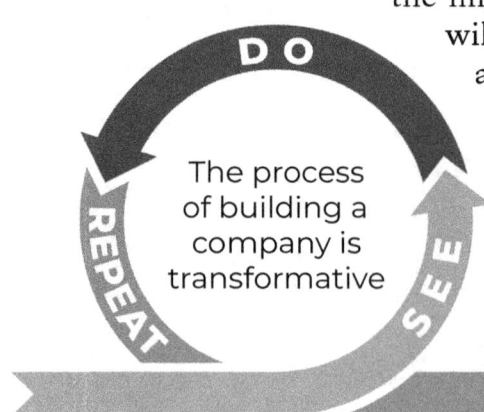

The process of building a company is transformative

will be joyful and fun, all of them will be meaningful in your entrepreneurial journey.

PRACTICE: LEARNING

SEE

The practice of entrepreneurship is about learning. What kind of learner are you? Do you learn best by taking direction from others? Or are you someone who learns best by trial and effort and by doing it yourself to see what happens? Do you prefer to learn alone, or are you someone who learns better in a more social setting? The first step in curating your own entrepreneurship education is self-awareness. Understanding how you learn best can enhance your ability to learn what you need to know.

DO

Conduct a skills gap analysis.

- Review the list of basic business skills in this chapter. Which topics are you comfortable with and which ones give you pause? Make a list of the subject areas where you believe some additional education could be helpful and do some research on where you might find credible educational programming.

- Take the EMP® or another personal mindset assessment and learn more about yourself and your own mindset. Are there mindset skills you would like to enhance or develop? Do the research, and find out where you can find help with building your own mindset.

REPEAT

Learning is naturally embedded into the practice of entrepreneurship. You will learn with every step and every action you take toward reaching your entrepreneurial goals. However, you can enhance the learning process with effort and self-awareness. Using the insights you have gained in the gap analysis exercise and your reflections on how you best learn, sit down and make a list of what you would like to learn more about right now. Make this a practice. Set aside thirty minutes once a week and review your entrepreneurial practice journal and identify one new subject area and see what you can learn that week.

Remember to consider the different ways you can learn. If you are a social learner, consider creating a mastermind group of others who want to learn about similar topics. Together you can collaborate on your learning and hold each other accountable. Or if you learn better with direction, maybe you want to seek out a coach or mentor to guide your learning and help ensure you are reaching your goals. If you are more of a solitary learner, you can find lots of content online and in books. Or if you learn better by doing, try to find an opportunity to work in an internship or take a job in an industry of interest. Figure out what works best and prioritize learning in your entrepreneurial practice.

CHAPTER 6

BUILDING YOUR NETWORK

Courage starts with showing up and letting ourselves be seen.
—Brene Brown

Woody Allen once famously said, "80% of success in life comes from showing up." On the other hand, Warren Buffet has said, "The difference between successful people and really successful people is that really successful people say 'no' to almost everything." These two quotes sum up the quandaries that perplex many entrepreneurs about networking.

How much time should you invest in building relationships and networking versus keeping your head down and getting work done? How do you connect with the right people instead of spending lots of time trying to attend every program and event available, just to come home with a bunch of contact information but nothing that really seems to fit your situation? Figuring out the answer to these questions and learning to master networking will make a defining difference in how successful you will be as an entrepreneur. Perhaps you are already a master networker or maybe you struggle with it. No matter where you are on this scale, be assured, networking is a skill that can be learned and improved upon. Before we discuss the importance and techniques of networking, let's take a look at your current network. How many of these statements are true for you?

- I have close friends and family I can count on when needed.
- I know a lot of people from all walks of life and of all ages and backgrounds.
- I am comfortable with meeting new people.
- I frequently talk to other people about my company.
- I am a good listener.
- I understand networking is about building relationships.
- I am available to help others.
- I am aware of the opportunities for meeting people in my community.
- I am aware of the associations and organizations that can help me with my business.

WHO SHOULD BE IN YOUR NETWORK?

There is almost an element of magic in the power of networking that can be thought of as being based on the power of numbers. We show up or talk to someone and, magically, we meet someone who can help us with a problem we are facing.

Brad Chisum, the entrepreneur we discussed earlier who was a co-founder of Lumedyne Technologies, tells the story of attending a student competition. His team didn't win but he met someone, who introduced him to someone, who ultimately became the key to his ability, to not only raise the money they needed at that time but also their acquisition by Google. He called this *serendipity*. According to Brad, it is because of this connection, he and his partner, James Hereford, started the Launch Factory, a program that matches entrepreneurs with opportunities. Brad and James say their goal with this initiative was to ignite serendipity for entrepreneurs, rather than leave it to chance.

I found this a fascinating perspective. The dictionary defines serendipity as "the occurrence and development of events by chance in a happy or beneficial way." When you check the thesaurus for synonyms for serendipity, you will find words such as *fluke*, *happenstance*, even *dumb luck*. So, how would the Launch Factory do this? Can we actually create serendipity?

In his book, *The Serendipity Mindset*, Christian Busch suggests that serendipity isn't about dumb luck or any kind of luck in the sense of randomness. He argues serendipity is about seeing links that others don't and combining them in a strategic way. Furthermore, in his book he shows examples of how serendipity works in all walks of life. Through these examples he provides suggestions for how anyone can enhance their prospects for serendipitous events that will help them reach their goals.

Similarly, in his book *The Medici Effect*, Frans Johansson also suggests innovation and opportunity come from the intersection of ideas, cultures, and concepts. Like the magic of the creative problem we discussed earlier, when you are focused on a problem or a need, and as you increase your interactions with people, you will find more connections and possibilities within which a solution will emerge. However, we can enhance the chances of getting to that solution or filling that need if we understand how to refine the scope and composition of our network.

Most entrepreneurs know they need to build their network, but it isn't always clear who should be in the network. We often refer to their network as their *social capital*. Social capital may

DO

Social capital may be considered even more important than financial capital for the entrepreneur.

REPEAT

SEE

be considered even more important than financial capital for the entrepreneur.

Contributions to our understanding of social networks theory and social capital has been an interdisciplinary effort, with research on networks going back some ninety years to the work of psychotherapist Jacob Moreno. He was one of the first social scientists to develop models of personal relationships. The field of social networks emerged some twenty years later when mathematical models were used to better understand relationships.

One study of significant importance to the domain of entrepreneurship was the work of Stanford sociologist Mark S. Granovetter. Grounding his work in network theory, Granovetter identified two types of relationships. Close or *strong ties* are the people in our intimate circle such as family and close friends. The second is *weak ties*. These are the relationships that we build among people who are not in our intimate circle. These are the people we know that we can reach out to on occasion, but we don't interact with them intimately like we do with family and friends. Weak ties may include a wide range of people, from school classmates or office mates to people we know from organizations like our church or the local chamber of commerce.

While entrepreneurs need strong ties that serve as support during challenging times, it is your network of weak ties that can contribute the most in helping you build and grow your entrepreneurial venture. The broader and more heterogeneous your network, the more access you will have to resources.

WHERE TO NETWORK?

Today most communities understand the importance of helping entrepreneurs build their network in their city. We often refer to these community efforts as entrepreneurial ecosystems. The idea of an entrepreneurial ecosystem is not new. In fact, one of the earliest examples might be found back in fifteenth century Florence, Italy, when the Medici banking family provided a location and financial support that would bring together artists and allow them to pursue innovation in the arts. Their patronage literally changed the world by providing a cultural bridge from the Middle Ages to the modern world, commonly known as the Renaissance, funding the work of the likes of Michelangelo and da Vinci.

Closer to home, the emergence of Silicon Valley in the mid-twentieth century is another example of an entrepreneurial ecosystem. Visionaries such as the "traitorous eight"—a group of engineers who left Shockley Semiconductor Laboratory and partnered with Arthur Rock, a young investment banker from New York—influenced some of the world's most influential companies, such as Apple and Intel.

About the time these technology founders from Silicon Valley were being elevated to rock star status, the age of the "creative class" and the millennial generation was born. The urgency to understand and imitate these high-growth business systems increased. Today, communities and countries throughout the world invest in building entrepreneurial ecosystems for a variety of reasons.

While business has long been viewed as an engine for economic growth and wealth creation and critical to gaining regional and national advantage, today, entrepreneurship is also viewed as a solution to social problems. It can provide the necessary emancipation to individuals to pursue freedom, independence, and escape the status quo. A high-performing entrepreneurial ecosystem leads to increased knowledge spillover and innovativeness, and the opportunities that emerge become influential in a region's ability to attract and retain the best and brightest talent.

The idea of an *ecosystem* is borrowed from the biological sciences and is defined by the dictionary as: ". . . a community of interacting organisms and their physical environment." Ecosystems are robust, scalable, and can solve complex dynamic problems. Any ecosystem has three components, the *community* (agents, non-agents, and nutrients), the *system* (how it works), and the *outcome* (a healthy sustainable place to exist).

The recipe for an entrepreneurial ecosystem is the same. Like bookends, the ingredients (the community) and the outcome (a vibrant economy) can be formulaically approached. Identify entrepreneurs (agents), add educational institutions and entrepreneurial support organizations (non-agents), and mix with investors (nutrients), and the desired outcome is a strong and vibrant economy. However, the real magic is in finding the formula for the system or interconnectedness that can provide the desired results. Let's look more closely at how this formula works and how an entrepreneur can use the principles of an ecosystem to build social capital.

Joe Hodges started working at a young age and enjoyed spending the fruits of his labor. Leveraging what he learned in his first job, Joe started a company with a partner. When the two of them began to have differing visions for the company, he agreed to leave the company and when he did, he signed a commonly used legal document wherein he agreed not to start another competing company within the next two years. Because of this agreement, often referred to as a *noncompete,* he took a job with a large insurance company, and this is where he found the inspiration for his next, much more successful venture.

At the time, he thought he had been an entrepreneurial failure. But in retrospect, what he found out was that by taking this position, he learned even more about his industry, and he was able to build a much larger network of contacts who would be vital to his success. It was this network that provided a bridge to a much bigger entrepreneurial success story when he started INETICO, a health care cost containment company he built and ultimately sold.

An entrepreneur can use the principles of an ecosystem to build social capital.

When he decided to launch the company, he did so with a few paying customers. However, as Joe puts it, he was young and had never focused on saving money. In fact, in order to launch this company, Joe put everything he had into the business. When he tells the story, he says he didn't even have money for food or shelter. But he was determined to bootstrap the business and so he initially even slept in a closet in the office space he rented. What he did have was passion and a great network.

One day, in the first few days of starting the company, Joe walked into a Chinese restaurant near his business and ordered lunch. Joe is an outgoing, talkative person and as he was ordering the food, he shared what he was doing with the owner. The owner had a similar story of hard work, and he told Joe of his own story of starting his company with nothing. As Joe tells the story, the owner said, "I am excited for you. We had help along the way, and this is what I want to do for you. Are you making any money yet?" When Joe said "no," the owner of the business told him he didn't want him to worry about food. He said, "I want you to show up here every day, and I am going to feed you. I want you to be here every day." That day the restaurant owner introduced Joe to all the staff and told them that when Joe comes in every day, you are to feed him whatever he orders, and he will not be expected to pay.

Now Joe had shelter and food. But the assistance he got didn't end there. Joe was talking with a friend one day about his new company. His friend asked if his prospective customers were all in the region. Joe told him this would be a national company, with customers in locations throughout the US. At the time, this friend worked for Southwest Airlines on the weekends as a flight attendant and had recently gotten a divorce. As a Southwest employee, he had a companion pass he could share with anyone he wanted, and since his divorce, he had no one with whom to share this pass. The friend told Joe, if this companion pass would help him, he could have it and fly standby on Southwest at no cost. So now, Joe could travel in an unlimited capacity and he had food and shelter. All because there were people along the way who saw his passion, believed in him, and wanted to help.

An entrepreneurial ecosystem relies on a sense of place to operate—i.e., the *community*. For Joe, it was critical to create both a community of experts in his field through his previous work experiences and a community of friends and supporters through his daily interactions in the city in which he lived. But when he launched INETICO in Tampa, Florida, in 2004, the programs to support entrepreneurship were limited. Today, like many cities, Tampa has a growing community of entrepreneurs, and, along with this growth, has been an increasing number of programs to support entrepreneurs.

About ten years after Joe started INETICO, a young female Hispanic entrepreneur Dr. Jacki Darna began her own entrepreneurial journey. Jacki was working in anesthesiology when she delivered her second child. After a difficult cesarean birth, she experienced dangerous prolonged nausea. As someone who believed in and studied natural medicine, Jacki sought a natural remedy. Having worked with her own patients and from her medical studies, she knew, pressure on the Chinese meridian point P6, named the Nei-Guan point, which is located on the inner arm near the wrist, can be used for the treatment of headaches, nausea, and vomiting. Around the same time, her stepmother brought her a peppermint plant after having read that smelling peppermint can help with nausea. Jacki combined the two for her own use, found that it worked, and went on to create nomonausea®, a natural remedy for nausea, headaches, and sleeplessness.

By the time Jacki started her company, there was a strong and growing number of programs to support startups. After pitching her company to the local chamber, Jacki launched her company out of their Startup Scholars program. When this program ended, she looked around and found an incubator program at the Lowth Entrepreneurship Center in the Sykes College of Business at the University of Tampa, where she worked for the next year. As a part of that program, she was able to tap into the faculty and network of the university and the entrepreneurship program to build her business model, her strategy, her brand, and customer base. She also gained access to university student talent and was able to hire interns to fill in her staffing needs at a very low cost. Together, these programs helped her move from idea to selling products. By the time she left the university program, she was not only selling products successfully on the internet but was also on the shelves of several well-known stores.

But she didn't stop with local programs; she soon learned there were many programs nationally, and even internationally, to help early-stage entrepreneurs. When she was attending a conference for continuing medical education, there was a conference of WBENC (the Women's Business Enterprise Council) in the same hotel. She decided to "crash" the conference and went into the exhibit hall to look around. She started talking to the people at the conference, and this is where she learned about becoming certified as a women-owned business, which she subsequently applied for and received. This certification provides access to a vast network of support, mentoring, and business opportunities, including increased visibility in corporate and government supply chains. Through this group, she was able to work with other female-owned businesses to reduce manufacturing costs and increase sales opportunities. She went on to become a finalist in the Pepsi Choice competition and many other programs designed to provide assistance and visibility to entrepreneurial companies.

Through this process, Jacki became an expert at pitching her concept. Anytime she met someone new, she was able to succinctly and concisely share her story. With Joe, it was much the same. He shared his story with passion and enthusiasm and developed meaningful relationships. However, they both also learned that networking is not just about gaining access to people and pitching a business, it is also about listening.

While building connections via the ecosystem is important, not all networking is equal when it comes to providing value to an entrepreneur. Valuable networking increases opportunities for strategic connections and provides feedback, information, customers, funding, and additional contacts. But many entrepreneurs tell me, while they know these programs and events exist, they don't know how to access them and which ones are worth their time. Strategic networking isn't always intuitive and can't be found at every event that is labeled as a meetup or networking program. Knowing how to interact professionally and with a planned approach takes some thought and planning. This is the magic of the *system*, e.g., how it operates.

HOW TO NETWORK

What are the key elements of *strategic networking*? The first is awareness and access. Gaining access to the local entrepreneurial ecosystem is the easiest place to start with this process. A simple internet search can often yield results. Sponsored programs like SCORE and SBDC ® programs discussed in earlier chapters are available in even small communities and can not only provide mentoring and assistance but also connections to other support programs.

Co-working spaces are also a great place to learn more about your local ecosystem. When you work in a co-working space, you may be expected to pay a small fee or buy a membership that will give you access to the space and other amenities such as food, drink, or technology. But the most important takeaway is often the like-minded people you may meet there. Beyond co-working spaces, you may have local incubator and accelerator programs that provide not only space but also education and access to an even more targeted group of people and resources.

Once you have gained access and honed your own pitch, one of the most important skills you can bring to this process is to learn to listen. Communication and relationship building involves both talking *and* listening. Strategic networking is more about listening and learning than it is about selling every conversation partner on what you know. But it also isn't about allowing yourself to be held captive by someone else's endless chatter. Knowing how to disconnect from a conversation is also an important skill.

For networking to provide real benefit, it is also important to find a way to record important names, contacts, and other information. In many cases, business cards, which used to be the norm, are no longer exchanged. The days of the index card in the jacket pocket are also mostly gone. Both have been replaced by the ubiquitous cell phone—good networkers figure out a way to literally take notes as needed to retain useful information. Strategic networking doesn't always involve a specific plan, it does involve making sure you take the time to move around the room and meet people. Talking to the same group of people you already knew before the event may be fun and if that is the goal, then by all means enjoy. But if you want to leave with more opportunities than you had before, remember to add some people to your "weak ties" group.

WHY ENTREPRENEURS NETWORK

Both Joe and Jacki reaped positive *outcomes* from their networking experiences. Through his efforts and with the support of his network, within three months of starting INETICO, Joe was in the black, and within six months, he was making enough money to not only pay for his food, airline tickets, and hotel rooms but also buy a home.

When Joe tells this story, he gets so excited and says he still cannot believe the experience of friendship and gifts that materialized when he needed it. He continues to marvel at their kindness that he will never forget and how they each contributed to his entrepreneurial dream. After seven years, he sold the company and was able to pursue a doctorate and move on to his new venture, which he runs today.

Today Jacki's company is in twelve countries and can be found in 30,000 big-box retail stores like CVS, Bed Bath & Beyond, and Buy Buy Baby, Walmart, and, of course, Amazon. They both built their companies without taking investment capital and have both demonstrated great market success. In turn, their success has contributed to the local network of entrepreneurs and to their field, a nice return on the investment of time and energy in building their business network.

PRACTICE: NETWORKING

SEE

Entrepreneurs don't let a lack of resources stop them. The ability to secure resources is a defining attribute of the practice of entrepreneurship. The network of individuals you know is one of the most important assets you have as an entrepreneur. Your social capital is even more important in many ways than financial capital because your network is often instrumental in helping you get the resources you need. How robust is your network? Do you have close ties with whom you can share the emotional and personal side of your entrepreneurial practice? Do you have a large diverse network of people who can help you gain access to everything else you need—people, capital, and access? How comfortable are you with networking? Does the mere thought of a networking event exhaust you? Or do you love to meet new people?

DO

Evaluate your network and your networking skills in relation to the concept or venture you are working on or an opportunity you would like to pursue. Look for gaps in your network. Consider how you approach networking. Reflect on any changes you need to make to build a network that will help you reach your goals. Now, do some research on your local entrepreneurial ecosystem. Although it is often hard to find everything, you will likely find many opportunities to fill in the gaps in your network. Now find one event and practice your strategic networking skills.

REPEAT

Create a networking plan using what you learned in your self-assessment, your ecosystem research, and your networking practice. Build in time to attend select events and programs in your community. Volunteer to help out with a local charity and, even better, serve on a charity board. You will not only learn more about organizational operations, but you may also be sitting around the board table with people whom you would otherwise be unable to access. When you meet someone new, focus on what you can learn about them. Everyone has a story, and you may be surprised to find someone who has access to exactly what you need. Reach out to someone you admire and see if you can take them to lunch or have coffee. Create opportunities for serendipity. Meeting new people and building and managing relationships requires practice and effort. Whether you are building a network for the first time or already have extensive social capital, strategic networking is an ongoing process. Networks need to be managed and evaluated over time. Include a strategic approach to networking into your entrepreneurial practice.

PART III
REPEATING

CHAPTER 7

RESILIENCE

I'm convinced that about half of what separates successful entrepreneurs from the non-successful ones is pure perseverance.

—Steve Jobs

In 2015, the University of Tampa decided to invest heavily in a space for student entrepreneurs to study and collaborate on their business concepts. As the program director there, I was fortunate enough to be involved in virtually all aspects of the design of the space. One of the tasks I had was to identify quotes for select locations on the walls that would inspire the aspiring entrepreneurs who would be studying and working in the space. The opening quote for this chapter was one we selected to be displayed prominently in the center.

We selected this quote because the willingness to achieve something, despite difficulties, failures, or opposition, is often what makes all the difference in whether an entrepreneur succeeds or ultimately fails. However, most successful entrepreneurs have something more. They not only persist in their entrepreneurial endeavor, but they are also resilient. That is, they rebound from difficulties and failures, and they learn from them. They, and their business concepts, are changed from challenges and failures and are even better because of them.

This is the third phase of the See, Do, Repeat practice of entrepreneurship. The ability to see opportunities and the willingness to act on them gets the entrepreneur to the starting line. But winning the race requires resilience. We aren't born with a "how-to" manual for life. There isn't a map that shows us how to navigate all the twists and turns and road junctures of life. The same is true for entrepreneurship.

There are many books, like this one, that can tell us about entrepreneurship. There are many people who will share their stories of entrepreneurship. In the end, it is only in the practice of entrepreneurship, the returning daily and executing past failure, that will allow you to reach your entrepreneurial vision. To do this, you will need to be resilient. Fortunately, resilience is a psychological skill you can build. But, as with all the skills we have been discussing in this book, you must know where you are before you can know how to improve. How many of the following are true for you?

- I try to respond rather than react to change.
- I believe that stress makes me stronger.
- Where possible I try to see the humorous side of situations.
- I am not easily discouraged.
- I view obstacles as the need to make changes in my plan.
- I usually have backup plans.

RESILIENCE AND ENTREPRENEURSHIP

Most people know about the famous entrepreneur Thomas Edison and his perspective on failure from the story about his experience with the light bulb. Credited with saying, "I didn't fail. I just found 2,000 ways not to make a light bulb: I only needed to find one way to make it work," Edison believed failure was just one more step toward success. However, many don't know that he also believed disability was simply a challenge to overcome. Edison loved music but he began to lose his hearing when he was only fourteen years old, after a severe illness. By middle age, he was completely deaf in one ear and 80% deaf in the other. Despite this disability, Edison gave us recorded sound when he invented the phonograph, based out of his work on the telegraph and telephone.

If you visit the Edison Museum in Fort Myers, Florida, you will see his personal phonograph is riddled with bitemarks. Edison overcame the challenge of extremely limited hearing by biting into the machine to "hear" the music through the vibration in his cheek and jaw. He was also actually able to select all the music sold by his company, through the same process, by biting into the piano as musicians auditioned.

There are plenty of stories about the failures of well-known entrepreneurs that demonstrate the importance of resilience. Take, for example, Traf-O-Data, Bill Gates' failed startup, was instrumental in teaching him important lessons needed to start Microsoft. Colonel Sanders' recipe was reportedly rejected by 1,000 restaurants before he started his own line of restaurants. Sir James Dyson created more than 5,000 prototype flops on the way to the development of his extremely successful Dyson vacuum.

From Bill Gates to the local shop owner, virtually all entrepreneurs have failed at one time or another along the pathway to success. Every entrepreneurial experience is an experiment. The very practice of entrepreneurship is about making and testing assumptions to reach a desired outcome. But along the way, outcomes will often not match expectations. At the same time, we know for successful entrepreneurs, ultimate failure is not an option. In order to persevere, every entrepreneur must have some measure of resilience.

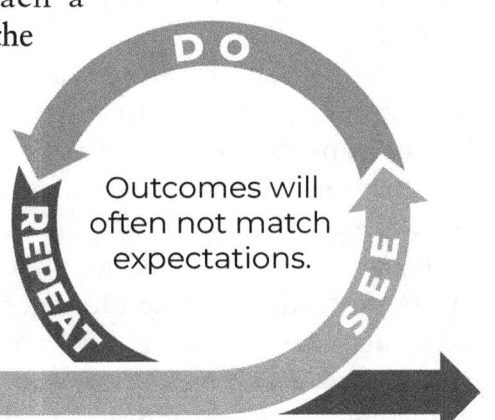

A few years ago, one of my graduate students dropped out of the entire graduate program, after angrily walking out of class during a spirited discussion on the role of failure in entrepreneurship. I had introduced the idea that failure is part of every journey of success, and failure can actually be a positive outcome in that it can illuminate the way forward. I also shared the idea of "failing fast" and how it is better to seek out what isn't working early on to save time and money. He became quite angry and said, "I can't believe you want us to fail. I came here to learn how to succeed." He then proceeded to walk out of class.

I didn't get the chance to talk to him again, so I can only speculate on why he was so angry with the discussion. However, it seemed that for him, failure was an outcome to be avoided at all costs. Since I couldn't confirm it was that classroom discussion that led to his withdrawal from the program, based on his remarks during the conversation, I was certain it played a role in his decision.

This experience left a strong impression on me. I felt I had somehow failed in communicating with this student. I already knew there was a mental health crisis on college campuses, that was at least in part driven by an exceptionally high need for achievement among our youth. Yet, where were we teaching skills associated with learning to cope with failure and challenge? Shouldn't resilience training be part of an education for all our students and especially for anyone who wanted to be an entrepreneur? This ultimately influenced me to begin to research resilience among successful entrepreneurs and to build a methodology for better preparing to rebound from failures, loss, and challenges.

Understanding resilience has become quite popular among social and natural scientists, in virtually all fields of study, from ecology to psychology to engineering. The term is used to describe the behavior of people, plant life, and materials. It has been used to examine and describe social systems as well as individuals.

Regardless of the field, our understanding of resilience is fairly constant. Resilience generally refers to a system of response and the ability to recover from uncontrollable outside disturbance or impact. It is a coping system that deals with the consequences of changes. Having its origin in the Latin *resiliens*, that is "to rebound or recoil," it implies a sense of elasticity. Psychologists who study resilience among people have suggested that, in life, it is not the nature of difficulties we face that matter, it is our ability to cope with these challenges.

But resilience isn't just about coping with the uninvited or unexpected. Theories of resilience also suggest an adaptive quality, that includes learning from disruption through the process of rebounding. Resiliency includes the ability to not only cope but to learn from difficulties. To be able to rebound to a better place than before.

We have already established that the practice of entrepreneurship requires recognizing and acting on opportunities. But, as Steve Jobs suggests in the opening quote for this chapter, the difference between those entrepreneurs who succeed and those who don't is perseverance. Because the world in which we operate is unpredictable and uncontrollable, our ability to persevere in a positive way requires building strong resiliency skills. In fact, in one study of first-time entrepreneurs in Canada, the businesses of those who were more resilient and, thus, better able to deal with the business challenges they faced were more successful and more likely to survive during the time period under study, than those with less resilient business owners.[25]

Starting with stories of how other entrepreneurs rebound in times of loss and failure can provide us with insight into how to be prepared for our own challenges. But knowing about resilience and rebounding from a setback is very different. One we can observe from a distance, but the other we feel personally and intensely. In the end, like any other skill, the way we learn to become resilient is through application and practice, that is, to experience loss and failure and setback. For any of us who have lived a few years, we have probably experienced failure and challenges from which we had to rebound. However, even when we've had a significant failure, remaining resilient during loss and failure is challenging. Beyond learning from the experiences of others, there are some very important ways to enhance your personal resilience and to build a resilient business.

BUILDING PERSONAL RESILIENCE

The ability to recover from outside impact includes three stages: readiness and preparedness, response and adaptation, and recovery and adjustment. Developing our own personal resilience requires that we prepare by considering the holistic nature of our being. Generally, there are four types of resilience we need to consider: physical, mental, emotional, and social. Resilience in any one of these requires strength, flexibility, and agility in the others. A starting point for resilience is our physical, mental, emotional, and social health.

Knowing and addressing your physical, mental, emotional, and social needs is one of the most important steps you can take to prepare yourself for the entrepreneurial journey. These may include not only getting the sleep, exercise, and nutrition you need but also taking time for friends and family and perhaps even very personal practices, like mindfulness through meditation, or social practices, such as engaging with your church or social group.

As we consider our own personal resilience, it can be helpful to reflect on times in our life when we were able to recover from challenges. Reminding ourselves of how we processed challenges in the past and how we successfully navigated through the difficult times can provide a window into our own personal coping behaviors. These past recoveries, no matter how small or seemingly insignificant, can be affirming and a powerful way to prepare for future loss and disruption.

In my own research on entrepreneurial resilience, there have been a few primary themes around how to cope with failure and challenge, and how to build resilience. The first is to

A starting point for resilience is our physical, mental, emotional, and social health *maintain mental agility*. This means having the ability to switch from reacting to responding to an outcome. Reacting is an opposite response, or an action in reverse, that is taken without much thought as to the end result. A response on the other hand involves stepping back, considering not only what happened but why, and then taking action based on this consideration. Second, and closely related, is to *reframe the way you think about failure*. When I ask many entrepreneurs how they think about failure, they say it is simply a lesson, a way to learn what you need to know, to build and grow a successful business.

For example, one young entrepreneur I know is trying to raise money (unsuccessfully at this stage) for a consumer product he has been working on for far too long. After nearly three years, he still hasn't been able to gain traction among his targeted customers. His problem has been a lack of mental agility and an inability to reframe failure. He has fallen in love with his product as it is. He continues to react to feedback, with more reasons why the product works rather than listening to the negative feedback, asking questions, and seeking even more input so he can improve or even abort this product and move on to something more marketable. Mental agility means not only the ability to move from reaction to response but to do so in a timely manner.

One way to ensure we are prepared to respond rather than to react, is to consider our options ahead of time. A third way entrepreneurs have reported they cope with challenges is to always have *backup plans,* a plan A, B, and C. This requires an innovation and opportunity mindset and a willingness to go with the flow of life. Fourth, most entrepreneurs also report they simply *don't accept failure as an option*. Failure probably means a change is required, but it doesn't mean stopping or giving up.

And, finally, always have *some part of your life you can control* when everything else feels out of control. People want to be in control. When we are not, we are under stress. Some stress can be helpful, if we are able to respond in a positive way, but excessive stress and being in a constant state of distress is dangerous, to both your personal health and your business.

Beyond your own personal resilience, it is important to think about how to build a more resilient business. One of the best examples of resilience in business is the story of Barefoot Wine. The entire company was started when plan A didn't work out.

When Bonnie Harvey couldn't collect on a debt she was owed by a winery in California, she sent in her then-boyfriend, Michael Houlihan, to help her get paid. When the owner convinced Michael he didn't have any money to pay, Michael looked around the facility and asked him what he was going to do with "[a]ll the wine he had in those barrels." Michael agreed to take the wine as payment. Then he and Bonnie had to do what they have always done best, turn lemons into lemonade, or in this case, turn wine in barrels into the best-selling wine in the US and a multimillion-dollar business they ultimately sold to E & J Gallo.

A RESILIENT VENTURE

A resilient business has four characteristics: *diversity, efficiency, adaptability,* and *cohesion*. First, diversity in your business means having multiple product lines where possible, multiple customer groups, backup plans, and multiple perspectives that can encourage more innovative leadership and decision-making. Second, efficiency in operations, especially in the early years, can literally be the key factor that allows a business to keep the doors open. We often refer to this as bootstrapping, that is, consuming modest resources wherever possible. Third, an adaptable business is one that can change in response to new pressures. Finally, a resilient business is unified in every way. That is, everyone in the business knows and believes in the mission and is willing to do what it takes to reach the goals of the venture.

In the building of Barefoot Wine, despite their lack of knowledge of the wine business, Bonnie and Michael knew how to remain personally resilient but also how to build a strong and resilient business. They were united in mission (cohesive) but had very different perspectives and styles (diversity). They understood how to bootstrap (efficiency) better than most any entrepreneurial team I have ever encountered. In fact, they started this business out of their laundry room and managed to conserve resources every step of the way. They listened to customers and vendors and were willing to change course (adaptable) any time it was necessary. In fact, the entire story of their startup is one of entrepreneurial resilience.[26]

Like Bonnie and Michael, every successful entrepreneur learns to not only cope with failure and challenge but to also rebound from them with positive outcomes. This is the power of resilience in entrepreneurship. You may have heard that there is often a silver lining to failure. In entrepreneurship, it is often gold. However, it is important to not let fear get in the way of this process. In the next chapter, we will take a closer look at the fear of failure.

PRACTICE: RESILIENCE

SEE

Like life, the practice of entrepreneurship includes good days and bad days. It includes highs and lows. There are days when every customer says "yes" and then there are days when you aren't sure you will be able to make payroll. There may be times when you are rejected by yet another prospective investor or are facing another failed product test. The ability to respond effectively, in all circumstances, is the differentiating factor in the successful practice of entrepreneurship. The three stages of resilience include being prepared, adapting, and recovering. Are you prepared? How ready are you physically, mentally, emotionally, and socially? Resilience in each of these requires strength and agility in the others. How prepared is your business for adversity? If you are already a practicing entrepreneur, have you considered how you can build diversity, efficiency, adaptability, and cohesiveness into your venture?

DO

In your entrepreneurial practice journal, consider your own resilience. Are there areas of your personal health you need to address? When you consider your own experiences with failure or extreme adversity, were you able to respond effectively? Reflect on what you learned. Were you able to incorporate those lessons into your life? Now consider your concept, venture, or current business. Are the elements of a resilient venture present in your plan or your organization? Use what you have written to make a list of changes you would like to make personally and in your venture.

REPEAT

Review what you have written in your entrepreneurial practice journal. The list of changes may be brief, or it may be very long. Either way, you don't have to do it all today. Remember, this is a practice. Even small changes to our understanding and readiness for resilience can make a difference when we are in the midst of extreme challenges. Find one area you would like to improve and add a ritual into your life that will do so. Perhaps there is even one change you can make today that would improve all the aspects of your health—physical, mental, emotional, and social? For example, would you benefit from a daily walk or some other physical activity with a good friend or someone else who can listen and provide encouragement and feedback? Walking is not only good for your physical health, but it can also engage you mentally, emotionally, and socially when you walk and talk with someone you trust and enjoy. Now take a look at your entrepreneurial venture. Does your practice and plan include the key features of a resilient business? Find one way to build in diversity, efficiency, adaptability, and cohesion. Keep notes on your personal and venture resilience and repeat this exercise regularly as part of your entrepreneurial practice.

CHAPTER 8

FEAR OF FAILURE

Success is not final; failure is not fatal:
it is the courage to continue that counts.

—Winston Churchill

The ability to persist and reach any kind of success in entrepreneurship lies in our willingness to execute past failure. For most of us, just reading or saying this word can lead to a queasy feeling in our stomachs. Thinking about failing often feels a bit like thinking about death. Fear is a survival instinct that is one of the most basic of human emotions. Fear helps protect us. Yet most of us know we often experience fear under conditions that are not truly dangerous to us. We imagine and project outcomes that never occur. We ruminate. Overcoming this kind of fear is about reframing how we think about it. It may even require changing how we define it. Overcoming a fear of failure requires awareness and acceptance. How many of the following apply to you?

- I recognize when I am afraid of failing.
- I understand why I am afraid of failing.
- I turn to others for a reality check when I am afraid.

- I believe failure can lead me to success by teaching me what I need to know.
- I am not easily discouraged by failure.

FEAR OF FAILURE AND ENTREPRENEURSHIP

Each fall for many years, I have been fortunate to be part of a team of scholars who teach in a program for entrepreneurship educators. This program, the Experiential Classroom, has become one of the leading seminar-type continuing education experiences for university and college entrepreneurship faculty and PhD students.

During the program, one of the most inspiring sessions focuses on how to captivate a classroom. In this talk, the professor shares what has worked for him over his long and storied career, teaching entrepreneurs both in the US and around the world. In his presentation, he addresses the fear most of us feel each time we are in front of an audience.

When he talks about the nervous feeling we get before we speak, he shows a picture of butterflies flying in formation. The butterflies are a physical response to our bodies and minds being "on-point." According to the professor, the goal is not to eliminate the butterflies, but to get them to fly in formation. In fact, he suggests, feeling anxious is a positive response because those butterflies are a reminder that if we focus the anxiety, we can be in the moment and completely attentive to the task at hand. What is especially powerful about this presentation is, throughout the presenter's life, he has been challenged with a stutter. Yet, when the butterflies align for him, the stutter disappears.

Throughout this book, we have talked about failure as a provider of lessons and a way to recognize that change is needed. We have also discussed the paradox entrepreneurs often feel with respect to failure. They know that failure is a part of every success, but they also know failure is not an option. The opening quote by Winston Churchill sums up this paradox well.

I think of this paradox with respect to two concepts: equifinality and resilience. The first, equifinality, is a concept I learned during my PhD days, and it has always been a favorite word for me. Equifinality is used a bit differently in the psychology literature, but in management theory, it simply refers to the belief that there are many paths to the same end, i.e., multiple ways to reach a final goal. In fact, a fatal flaw among many founders is assuming the solution they have created to address a problem in the marketplace is the most effective or efficient or is even desired by the marketplace.

The second, resilience, the capacity to recover quickly from difficulties, is required of a founder when they learn through trial and error that what they thought was true is not. This is the essence of the entrepreneurial theory of "fail early and fail fast." The less invested, the easier it is to pivot or adapt. Thus, failure may come along the way, but the final outcome can still be success. Reframing failure reminds us that we have options, and we can change the way we think about this concept and that each failure is a learning process. While maybe not welcome at the time, it can lead to ever-greater success than imagined.

As with public speaking, getting rid of our fear of failure is not the goal for any aspiring or practicing entrepreneur. However, ignoring the fear is not healthy and is also not recommended. Ignored anxiety just tends to build. Instead, recognizing fear and using what we learn from it, can be empowering and even valuable to our success. This is true for what many argue is the greatest fear facing every entrepreneur: the fear of failure. Let's look a bit more closely at failure and our fears associated with it and how to use them to our advantage.

REDEFINING FAILURE

Failure simply refers to outcomes that are not expected. We may think of failure as a lack of success. There are varying numbers of reports of business failures which may range from 20% to 80% or more. The reason for the large variance is because it is very difficult to define business failure.

The United States Bureau of Labor Statistics provides one of the most consistent reports. They define births and deaths of business firms based on quarterly reports of employee numbers. Their data suggests business failure rates are fairly consistent year to year. They report that about 20% of US small businesses fail within the first year, but by the end of year five, roughly 50% have faltered. After ten years, only around a third of businesses have survived.

Of course, these data do not include a solo entrepreneur since they are based on employee numbers. They also do not report the personal failures some entrepreneurs feel when they are removed or feel forced to leave their company by a partner or an investor. But they are a harsh reminder that failure is going to be the outcome for many business founders each year.

Every new business founder feels the stress of the unknown, and underneath all the variables, both controllable and uncontrollable, is the fear of not getting it right, or failing. Deciding to take this step into the unknown as an entrepreneur opens the founder to a high level of vulnerability. Failure is very personal for the entrepreneur. However, the starting of a business is not only a very personal activity, but also a very social one. At its core, the fear of failure is tied to potential feelings of shame and humiliation caused by failure. A business failure could leave us feeling like a personal failure. Fear of failing in business can mean a direct threat to our feeling of self-worth.

Interestingly, failure was not always defined in such personal terms. In fact, earlier usage of the word was tied solely to business. Failure has always been a necessary part of progress in life and business. The history of America is about entrepreneurs and entrepreneurship. This includes both their success and failures.

In the prologue of his fascinating book, *Born Losers*, Professor Scott Sandage chronicles the route the term failure has taken in the US from being a term associated with business to one that is now used to define us personally. Before the Civil War, failure commonly meant "breaking in business," that is, going broke. It was a banking and business term. However, he notes in this book, that by the dawn of the twentieth century, failure had become personal. Headlines suggesting people could quickly become "a nobody" and that the fear of failure had become the "bane of young men and women" were appearing. "Failure had become, what remains in the new millennium: the most damning incarnation of the connection between achievement and personal identity. 'I feel like a failure.' The expression comes so naturally, we forget it is a figure of speech: the language of business applied to the soul." [27]

No wonder so many people are afraid of entrepreneurship. Just this week, I had a conversation with a top CEO who is running a five billion dollar business but has a strong desire to try something "on his own." However, he continued to tell me that while he isn't afraid of much, the thought of taking the leap into entrepreneurship "scares him to death." Interesting use of the phrase. How often do we associate the potential of failure in something with the ultimate end, death?

Obviously, this shift in the definition of a business failure to a personal one has had vast implications for entrepreneurship. How many talented business leaders have foregone the entrepreneurial path because they were afraid of failing? How many strong business opportunities were missed because of the fear of failure? One study of 127 top management decision-makers in technology companies, where opportunities are presented in strong measure on a regular basis, found that fear of failure not only affects the willingness to act on opportunity, but it can also have an impact on our ability to even recognize an opportunity.[28]

Yet, despite the stories of the inhibiting effect of the fear of failure on many people, there are others who report that fear of failure has been a primary motivating factor in their entrepreneurial journey. For some, it turns out, the fear of failure can be turned into a force that drives them to success. Several years ago, I invited a very successful business owner into my class to talk to my students about his entrepreneurial journey. After telling his story of hard work and effort, he concluded with a heartfelt confession: he admitted to the students that he had been and is still often driven by a fear of failure. But he decided early on to use failure to his advantage.

Ray Ingersoll is another successful entrepreneur who, very early in his career, learned to turn his fear of failing, into a formula for success. Ray is the founder and CEO of The Ingersoll Group, an international sales, consulting, and training firm. But his first job may be the one that helped him prepare to build an international company that could win the business of industry giants such AT&T, Google, Delta, Mazda, and Pfizer.

Ray calls his philosophy about failure "the power of no." Ray's first job was cold calling long-distance calling services. The challenge with cold calling is that you are trying to sell something to someone who hasn't invited you to make a pitch. Cold calling is extremely difficult and means you are literally failing in your attempt to sell a product much more frequently than you are successfully closing a deal. Over time, what Ray learned from that experience was how many calls he had to make before he actually sold his product. He began to use that formula to change the way he thought about failing. He knew, if on average, he made ten calls before he made one sale that would pay him ten dollars in commission, then each time he received a "no" he would thank them for the one dollar contribution to his next sale.

He says he continues to use this reframing of failure in his business today. And, he has also learned that it is in the failure, when a prospective customer refuses his product, that he learns the most. Today his firm will actually pay clients who turn them down to spend some time talking with them about why they rejected their offer.

Every entrepreneur will face failure and rejection. Virtually every story of entrepreneurship has a good measure. Yet, successful entrepreneurs persist. Like Ray Ingersoll, they have developed methods for using fear to their advantage. How does this typically work?

MOVING BEYOND FEAR OF FAILURE

The first step is to *recognize your fear of failing*, own it, and name it. There are typically five components of fear. These include (a) experiencing shame and embarrassment, (b) devaluing one's self-estimate, (c) losing social influence, (d) having an uncertain future, and (e) upsetting important others.

Among entrepreneurs, one study found seven common failure fears: financial security, personal ability, ability to finance the venture, potential of the idea, social esteem, venture's ability to execute, and opportunity costs. These include common worries such as:

- Will I lose my money?
- Will I lose money that others have loaned or invested?
- Will I let others down?
- Will I lose the affection or support of my family and/or friends?
- Will I be embarrassed?
- Will this business fail?
- Will I have wasted my time on this venture?

Once you have owned your fears, you are then able to use this as a *reality check*. It is important to recognize this experience as an opportunity to slow down for a bit of reflection. During this reflection, you can ask yourself some important questions:

- Is my fear real?
- How real?
- Can I talk this over with someone to get perspective?
- What's the worst that can happen?

One successful entrepreneur once told me bad news is like a banana. As it ripens it also rots. Keeping bad news from yourself, and others who might be able to help you turn around your problem, is a dangerous practice. However, it is a common problem for many entrepreneurs. Why? Because it is easy to believe that if you just work harder or make another change, you will be able to address the problem before anyone else finds out. Yet, this seldom works. It is far better to recognize your fears right away and check to see if the problem is real. This will reduce rumination and worry (which is a drain on your energy) and make it much more likely to determine whether this is a real problem, or one that you are inventing mentally.

Having someone to turn to in times of fear, has become the first line of defense for Rupak Doshi, co-founder of OmniSync. His software platform guides entrepreneurs through step-by-step execution of essential projects that stem from the overall mission of raising funds to launch and scale their companies. At a young age, Rupak is already a serial entrepreneur. When I talked with him about how he deals with his fears of failure, he admitted his first reaction to failure is anger.

For many, anger is a common way to deal with fear. Fear leaves us feeling out of control, and anger can be one way to bring a bit of control back into the relationship. Rupak recognized this tendency when he was in graduate school. He had a lab mate who would always take him aside and help him calm down when his fears led him to anger. He learned to appreciate this because it kept him from lashing out and perhaps making the situation worse. So, when he and his partner in OmniSync lost a partnership that was vital to OmniSync and put the company at risk, Rupak's first response was anger. His partner, however, was his calming agent, and after they talked, they both realized they had a plan B, which according to Rupak, turned out to be an improvement over the original course of action.

Having *an alternative plan* is empowering. Considering and conceiving not only a plan B but also a plan C can help alleviate worry and allow you to direct your energy into the tasks at hand in your business. Thinking through what these alternative plans mean and simply knowing you have options can make all the difference. And, in the end, for the successful entrepreneur, it is about continuing the journey, not the failures along the way.

Benson Riseman is an incredibly successful entrepreneur who went from a challenging childhood to becoming the co-founder of Green Dot, the world's largest prepaid debit card company. When I talked to Benson about fear of failure, he had plenty of stories that sounded like they were right out of a movie. Epic failures he and his partner acknowledged, worked through, and found a way to continue toward their goal of building a company, which is now traded on the NYSE.

According to Benson, "What I have learned for sure in business is that 95% of the time, no matter what you think it will cost to accomplish something in business, it will cost more; no matter how much time you think it will take to accomplish something in business, it will take longer; and no matter what you think your business will be when you start it, it will be something different. Rather than digging in my heels and saying it has to be this way or it's a failure, it's like, no, if I have to keep failing until it feels right then I will because that is what the goal is—not to stop."

For entrepreneurs, the goal is to execute past their failures. This is just the way of innovation. The more epic your innovation, the more epic your failures are likely to be. Building in extra time, money, and support, can go a long way in helping you deal with the fear of failure. In the next chapter, we will look at the role optimism plays in this process.

PRACTICE: OVERCOMING FEAR OF FAILURE

SEE

Failure is an inevitable part of any success story. It is one of the best teachers we will ever have. Big opportunities are also usually accompanied by big failures. Entrepreneurs who reach their entrepreneurial goals have learned to execute past failure. Acknowledging our fears associated with failure, sharing them with others to get perspective, and redefining the role of failure in entrepreneurship is how we can be prepared to do this ourselves.

DO

In your entrepreneurial practice journal, reflect on your fear of failure. How do you define failure? Does failure feel final and fatal to you? What scares you about your entrepreneurial endeavors? Make a list of your deepest fears. Be honest and as specific as possible about them. Now make a list of all the previous times you were afraid of failing. Can you think of times that you were scared but went ahead and tried? How did that feel? Can you think of times when you were able to rebound from failure? Can you think of times when you gave up? Reflect on the role your fears have played in your entrepreneurial practice thus far. What would you do if you were not afraid? Have you been holding back on your dreams because of a fear of failure?

REPEAT

Identify one goal that will help you reach your entrepreneurial dreams that you haven't yet pursued due to a fear of failing.

- Honestly and openly share your goal and your fear with a trusted colleague or mentor and get their feedback.
- Develop a plan B and perhaps even a plan C in case your initial fears are realized and you need to adapt.
- Now go pursue that goal.

Keep notes and reflect on the entire process. Use the lessons you have learned and repeat this exercise regularly in your entrepreneurial practice.

CHAPTER 9

OPTIMISM

Optimism is the faith that leads to achievement.
Nothing can be done without hope and confidence.

—Helen Keller

While there are numerous definitions of entrepreneurship, virtually all of them include taking an action today, to create an outcome tomorrow. What is your general tendency when you think about the future? Are you more likely to agree with the first set of statements below or the second set?

- In uncertain times, I usually expect the best.
- I expect things to go my way.
- I don't get upset too easily.
- Overall, I expect more good things to happen to me than bad.
- If something can go wrong for me, it will.
- I hardly ever expect things to go my way.
- I rarely count on good things happening to me.

An underlying theme, of the practice of entrepreneurship is a focus on the future and a steadfast belief that what lies ahead will be good. In fact, it is this focus on the future that drives every entrepreneurial practice. This tendency to look forward through a positive lens has been a consistent theme in my interviews with hundreds of entrepreneurs over the years. And it makes sense. If not for reaching for a better future, why would anyone ever take on the work of entrepreneurship?

Yet not every successful entrepreneur I have interviewed or worked with over the years ranked themselves high on optimism. In fact, some have steadfastly argued that it was their cautiousness, and even skepticism at times, about the future that led to their success. Optimism clearly plays a role in the practice of entrepreneurship, but what specifically is the relationship between entrepreneurship and optimism?

UNDERSTANDING OPTIMISM

The role of optimism in entrepreneurship has been the focus of social scientists for many years. Like my own work, the results of this research have been mixed. Studies have demonstrated that dispositional optimism can enhance all three of the competencies in the See, Do, Repeat practice: the ability to recognize opportunities, the willingness to execute on those, and the propensity to persist.

Perhaps even more importantly, research has shown that optimism actually leads to more successful outcomes for entrepreneurial ventures.[29]

On the other hand, research has also shown that optimistic tendencies can be dangerous for entrepreneurs. These studies found optimism can leave

DO

REPEAT

SEE

Taking an action today, to create an outcome tomorrow.

you blind to the true costs and consequences of a situation or a decision and lead to poor decision-making.[30]

One of the challenges with optimism research, has been in how the term optimism has been defined. The word has its origins in the Latin *optimum,* meaning the best thing. Life, and any new venture, is full of uncertainty, and the way we approach decision-making can be thought of on a continuum. It is in the continuum we can find answers to the relationship between entrepreneurship and optimism. At each extreme is an optimistic view of the future and the other is a pessimistic one.

An optimist believes that whatever happens is the best outcome, even when it isn't what we expected or wanted. It is going with the flow, trusting in the universe. A pessimist, on the other hand, believes that my decisions are always ill-fated, and no matter what I do, the outcome will be bad. Psychologists use the term dispositional to refer to the tendency in a person to respond to situations in a predictable way. Dispositional optimism refers to the generalized, relatively stable expectation of good outcomes. Some people refer to this tendency as positive anticipation.

Over the years, as I have interviewed and talked to successful entrepreneurs, this tendency to anticipate the positive has been a common theme. This doesn't mean they are unrealistic or they don't have times when they are frustrated, angry, disappointed, or sad. It also doesn't mean they ignore the bad stuff. In fact, they do just the opposite. They are very grounded in reality. In his best-selling book, *The Power of Optimism*, Alan Loy McGinnis outlines the empowering characteristics of optimists. Among these is the ability to balance a trust that they have control over their future, while accepting what cannot be changed. He also suggests that optimists are seldom surprised by trouble. They understand their pathway will not always be smooth.

Returning to the optimism scale, there are others who may be thought of as being unrealistically optimistic. This tendency toward being overly optimistic has been shown to be a factor in both starting unsuccessful ventures as well as continuing unsuccessful ventures far too long. It has also been shown to be a factor in poor decision-making, with respect to financing business ventures.[31] Overly optimistic people tend to ignore data and don't accept reality. I have witnessed this among many very early-stage entrepreneurs and students, with whom I have worked over the years. This is understandable in many ways. However, taking a Quixotic approach of remaining wildly optimistic while ignoring reality will lead to wasted time and money and will get in the way of your entrepreneurial practice.

OPTIMISM AND THE PRACTICE OF ENTREPRENEURSHIP

Optimism plays a vital role in seeing opportunities. Optimists tend to employ mental activity that actually supports many of the skills necessary for opportunity recognition. Studies by neuroscientists have demonstrated the optimist's brain tends to engage in projecting positive future events and regularly use their imaginations to rehearse success.[32]

Other research has suggested that optimists are more likely to find innovative solutions and they allow for regular renewal, another practice which aids with the creative problem-solving process. Optimists tend to be more likely to allow for partial solutions, that is, they are more likely to keep pivoting until they get to the best solutions to customer problems. Optimism supports the ability to find and recognize opportunities. As Winston Churchill is credited with saying, "A pessimist sees the difficulty in every opportunity; an optimist sees the opportunity in every difficulty."

Nothing happens until thoughts are turned into action. Given their more positive view of the future, it is not surprising that optimists are more likely to be willing to take action than pessimists. Research has demonstrated that optimists are more likely to take the risk of investing their time and money into a new venture because they have a higher belief in positive returns from their actions.[33]

As we discussed earlier, fear of failure often discourages action. On the other hand, optimism reduces these fears because optimists tend to have higher levels of self-efficacy, that is, they believe they can impact their future. They also hold a more favorable view of the future and therefore they tend to have a higher sense of urgency for the future.

Dispositional optimism has also been shown to be correlated with a stronger sense of self-confidence in the ability to stretch and to accomplish what is needed to reach desired goals. Research has shown optimists tend to be less likely to be immobilized by uncertainty and they have an almost unlimited belief in their ability to keep growing and stretching. Optimism encourages action. In fact, without optimism, entrepreneurship would be less likely to ever occur. In one study of new business founders, a remarkable 33% of new business owners assessed their odds of success at ten out of ten. Only 4% assessed the odds to be less than five out of ten.[34]

Optimism leads to greater persistence and resilience. Optimists have been shown to have better-coping strategies, to be better able to adapt to problems and change, to have lower levels of anxiety and depression, and to be more likely to demonstrate high levels of resilience in the face of adversity. The expectation of positive outcomes that is at the core of dispositional optimism, has also been shown to facilitate continuous investment in the business and to lead to the ability to persevere in difficult times.

OPTIMISM AS A SKILL

We have made a strong case for optimism, and you may find yourself a bit discouraged if you are not naturally optimistic. But interestingly, psychologists suggest you can learn to be more optimistic. Learned optimism, often thought of as the opposite of learned helplessness, begins with awareness of the way we think about life and how we approach taking risks and

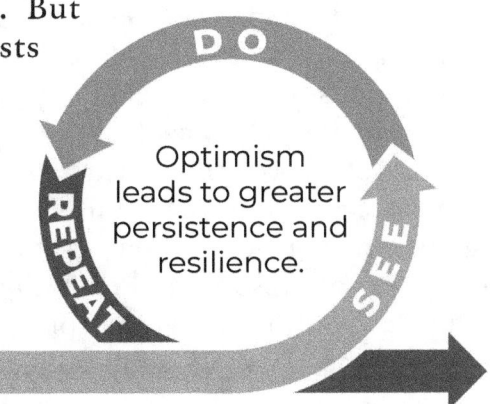

Optimism leads to greater persistence and resilience.

making decisions. Learned optimism has been championed by several psychologists[35] and is the process of recognizing and challenging pessimistic thoughts in order to develop a more positive approach. While you may not be a natural optimist nor ever become one, awareness of where you are on the optimism-pessimism continuum is important if you want to employ an entrepreneurial mindset.

Psychologists have identified three different ways we view the experiences that can impact where we may land on the pessimism to optimism scale. These three include personalization, pervasiveness, and permanence. We can learn to be more optimistic by reflecting on these three and how we approach situations in our life and work.

PERSONALIZATION

Personalization is how we view experiences, with respect to the role we play in the outcomes, specifically, whether we attribute a specific outcome to something internal to us or to something external to us. For example, a question you may ask yourself is whether you are able to clearly differentiate between when you are responsible and when you aren't, and how much responsibility you should take in each outcome? Optimists tend to be able to do this well. They don't take responsibility for issues beyond their control.

Recently I was talking with a group of female executives about female leadership, and they asked me how I deal with difficult conversations in the workplace. I told them I have learned to not take responsibility for the other person's reaction or response to our discussion. This hasn't always come easy for me, as someone who has often been challenged with a desire to please others. What I have learned is to focus on what I can control, that is, doing my best to engage in a conversation that was based, at least on my side, with respect and empathy, and delivered in a positive manner. If, at the end of the conversation, I am convinced I did my best, then I can let go of their response or reaction.

The same is true in business. If we do our best and still fail, an optimist will believe that whatever happens will eventually be for the best, even if it is not comfortable right now. Reflecting on where we attribute blame and how we respond to that perspective can help us learn to be more optimistic.

PERVASIVENESS

Pervasiveness refers to whether we view an unfavorable outcome as applicable to our entire life or whether we can apply context in our assessment. Pessimists tend to think when they experience failure, say in their business, that it should be applied to all aspects of their life. For example, I haven't made any sales this week, so I am a bad person, and therefore I am unlovable, and my family is likely to leave me. This kind of thinking isn't productive nor does it lend itself to being able to assess the reality of the situation.

Sometimes, despite our hard work, the outcome isn't what we want. In these cases, an optimist can turn to areas of their life that are working and find perspective and comfort there. Then they can return with renewed energy, to respond in a positive and productive manner to the situation. For those who tend to be more pessimistic, not letting failures and bad outcomes spill over into the future can lead to a more optimistic perspective.

PERMANENCE

Permanence is about whether we view a bad outcome as permanent or temporary. For the pessimist, a week of failed sales calls means the business will fail and it is time to give up. On the other hand, an optimist, with a positive view of the future, will be able to move beyond failure. Instead, they will be able to view the situation as a chance to learn more about how to succeed and try to figure out how to make the next sales call work with what they have learned. For any entrepreneur, it is important to keep failures and bad outcomes in perspective and not let them spill over into the future.

Reflecting on your own mental patterns, with respect to personalization, pervasiveness, and permanence, has been shown to be an effective way to move toward a more optimistic perspective. One method of approaching the process is to use a reflection method referred to as the ABC Technique.[36] When you find you are experiencing a negative outcome or experience, reflect on your self-talk related to the (A) adversity, your (B) beliefs, and the (C) consequences.

For example:

The Pessimist:

    A. Adversity: Our prospective investor turned us down.

    B. Beliefs: My product is bad, and I am no good at this.

    C. Consequences: You decide to give up.

The Optimist:

    A. Adversity: Our prospective investor turned us down.

    B. Beliefs: This investor is not the right fit and/or we may need to make some changes.

    C. Consequences: What did we learn, and how we can do better next time?

GRATITUDE

Practicing gratitude has been shown to be a way to change your perspective on what lies ahead. Gratitude can change the way we think and the way we view the future. Expressing gratitude causes our brains to release dopamine and serotonin which in turn make us feel better immediately.

Keeping a gratitude journal has even been shown to increase optimism.[37] Being grateful also grounds us in reality. My first entrepreneurial role model, my mother, taught me a great deal about the power of gratitude. During her life, she had to deal with great adversity. However, what I remember the most about my mother is her optimism, which she learned from her father, my grandfather. These were two of the most positive people I have ever known. And it was that optimism which gave her the courage to take bold steps and approach every aspect of her life with the mind of an entrepreneur.

FINDING A BALANCE

The practice of entrepreneurship will provide lessons and the opportunity to grow each step of the way. Those lessons come in the form of energy. Energy is neither good nor bad. We may process it as positive (a new opportunity) or negative (fear caused by a pandemic that closes the economy for months), but in the end, it is neither good nor bad because both can bring important transformation.

Our response to both the positive and negative reflects the degree to which we are centered. Are we able to stay focused on what is most important and not get carried too far off our path by either the positive or the negative energy? That is the test of balanced optimism. Our approach to life and decision-making will vary. There may be times when you lean toward extreme optimism, and this may be necessary to get you through challenging times. On the other hand, there are times you will need to step back and take a more calculating approach to decision-making. But in the long run, consistently extreme optimism or extreme pessimism will be detrimental to your practice and to your health. The successful practice of entrepreneurship includes balanced optimism, that is, a perspective which leans toward the positive but is grounded and realistic.

PRACTICE: OPTIMISM

SEE

Optimists hold a positive view of the future, and they understand everything is constantly changing. Because of this, they tend to be more comfortable with the uncertainty and ambiguity of entrepreneurship. They are willing to take action to realize their positive beliefs about the future. Optimists are more willing to keep going, even when the going gets tough. When they struggle with the future, they are willing to turn to others for help. Optimism is a skill and a practice that can be learned.

DO

Conduct an optimism mindset analysis. Using the ABC Technique described in this chapter, consider your own level of optimism. What does your self-talk tell you about where you fall on the pessimist to optimist scale? Answer these questions in your entrepreneurial practice journal. Do you find your level of optimism helps or hurts you in your entrepreneurial practice?

REPEAT

Based on what you learned from your analysis, consider whether your entrepreneurial practice would be enhanced by directing more attention to your self-talk and expectations. If it suggested your level of optimism is getting in the way of your entrepreneurial practice, you might consider these changes, to move the needle:

- If you found that you're making poor decisions based on unrealistic and overly optimistic projections, consider making it a practice to talk over your expectations with your mentor to get a more realistic perspective.

- If you are missing opportunities or not taking action because you are overly cautious and negative about the future, consider incorporating some of the learned optimism tools, such as a gratitude journal or using the ABC Technique to challenge your self-talk.

CHAPTER 10

CHOOSE YOURSELF

You can choose yourself. And you can say I am going to be successful, because I have decided I am going to be successful.

—Jeff Civilico

Entrepreneurship is empowering and transformative. It is also democratic. I fell in love with entrepreneurship education because I saw the power it has to transform lives and people on so many levels. As so many of the entrepreneurial stories shared in the book have shown, entrepreneurship can provide a pathway to income and wealth, for anyone who wants to invest in the practice.

Entrepreneurship doesn't require a specific degree or experience, and it doesn't discriminate by age or demographic. Entrepreneurship is available to anyone. It can be practiced on a very small and intimate scale, or it can be pursued as a change agent for the world. It can be practiced within an organizational environment or be a venue for creating a new organization. It can be applied in a not-for-profit environment, or it can provide extreme wealth. A single entrepreneurial effort can provide one job or thousands of jobs.

The practice of entrepreneurship is transformative to anyone who chooses to take the journey, and it is also a pathway to changing the world. Regardless of how it is applied, the principles of entrepreneurship remain the same. It is a learning and doing practice, that is skill-based. The goal is not mastery of every aspect, the goal is to keep learning and to execute past failure to reach your definition of success.

PASSION AND ENTREPRENEURSHIP

The practice of entrepreneurship requires total commitment and lots of hard work. This is one of the key lessons I have learned from years of working with entrepreneurs and from my personal experience. Certainly, it is possible to test a new opportunity and to try out an idea but to reach a big goal requires a big commitment. Only you can decide how big your goal will be. Only you can decide what kind of commitment you will make. But make no mistake, the practice of entrepreneurship is about choosing to pursue your dreams, not those of someone else. It is about choosing your own destiny, not one someone else creates for you. The practice of entrepreneurship is about passion, and it is about finding your passion. Without passion, all the hard work and commitment required may well be too much to endure.

Passion is one of the most evoked terms when people talk about entrepreneurship. There are countless studies that have confirmed the role of passion, in the motivation and intention to pursue entrepreneurship and the ability to persist in the face of challenges. The entrepreneurs I have worked with and interviewed have all been passionate about their entrepreneurial journey. For some, it was a passion for a product or industry.

DO

REPEAT

SEE

But to reach a big goal requires a big commitment

For others, it was enthusiasm for conducting business. For most, it was a desire to make a difference and the sheer joy of reaching for and achieving a big goal. For virtually all of them, passion was what gave them the stamina to keep going.

Many of my students tell me they know they need to pursue their passion if they want to succeed in their entrepreneurial practice, but they haven't yet discovered what they love enough to make the required investment. This is not surprising. My response to those students is to go out and live the practice of entrepreneurship and see what happens. Often, our passion will find us. And much of the time it may even surprise us.

When he was a young man, Jeff Civilico fell in love with juggling. It wasn't so much the act of juggling that he enjoyed. He loved the way people who watched him seemed to feel. They were smiling and laughing. His performances seemed to bring joy to others. So, he would juggle anything he could pick up around his house, often much to the chagrin of his mother and grandmother!

Jeff continued to juggle for fun and the occasional performance while he went to Georgetown University. After school, while the rest of his friends went on to pursue professional careers as corporate lawyers, bankers, or doctors, Jeff decided to pursue a different path. With a lot of hard work, Jeff turned his passion for performance into a career and his highly acclaimed Vegas shows have been three-time winners of the "Best of Las Vegas" awards and has been named one of the "Top Ten Things to Do in Vegas."

But performing in one of the top show cities in the world wasn't enough. Jeff is someone who practices the See, Do, Repeat model. He also has created a thriving business doing corporate entertainment and a philanthropic performance business, Win Win Entertainment, a national nonprofit that brings smiles to the faces of children by arranging in-person and virtual visits from entertainers, athletes, and celebrities.

When I had the chance to interview Jeff about his entrepreneurial career as a performer, we talked about the challenges of this vocation. Performance can be anything but democratic. There are thousands of talented performers who are finding ways to make money elsewhere because they have not been able to attain a coveted role as a performer. For many years performance meant you had to be discovered. But Jeff, and others like him, those with an entrepreneurial mindset, always find a way.

Jeff looked for opportunities, took action, and persisted through many challenges, some that could have destroyed his career had he let them. Even during the pandemic, which closed in-person performances, Jeff found a way to offer performances, corporate entertainment, and juggling lessons virtually. Jeff decided early on to pursue his passion, even though it was a far cry from what might have been expected of him, and he decided to choose himself and not wait to be chosen.

UNDERSTANDING YOUR WHY

Several years ago, one of my students was addressing an incoming freshman class at the university. His presentation was designed to give them information about entrepreneurship and to share his story about why he had chosen it as his major. He said, growing up he heard his father complain about his job and more recently he had seen his father lose his job. Sadly, his father was older and less employable than many others, who were also seeking employment in this field. He didn't want to find himself in that same position, so he decided to become his own boss.

This story reminded me of a friend, who said something similar to me. After twenty years of building a very successful company and then selling it, I asked her what her motivation for a career as a business owner had been. She told me she had watched both of her parents lose their jobs late in life, and she decided she would rather control her destiny than put it in someone else's hands.

I hear this a lot from my students. They are choosing themselves. Does this mean they are all going to be business owners? Not necessarily. Deciding to pursue business ownership is not for everyone. It is hard work, and it is all-consuming. Work-life balance is often out of the question. However, choosing yourself by applying an entrepreneurial mindset and using the See, Do, Repeat model, in your work and life, is an option for anyone.

WHAT CHOOSING YOURSELF REALLY MEANS

The practice of entrepreneurship must be about choosing yourself. Your dreams, your passion, your vision of your life. The practice of entrepreneurship is about being true to who you are. It is about living true to your values and taking advantage of your strengths and talents. But that does not suggest the practice of entrepreneurship is a selfish one.

Being an entrepreneur can be a thankless and often lonely job. As the founder of your venture, it is up to you to make sure the needs of the rest of the team are taken care of before your own. Like the captain of the ship, an entrepreneur is the final say in difficult decisions and is the last one to go home and the last one off when the ship is sinking. The responsibility and challenge can be exhilarating, and it can be overwhelming.

Many people begin an entrepreneurial practice knowing this, but along the way, they may forget. They forget because the busyness of an entrepreneurial practice gets in the way. The list of jobs to be done and tasks to be completed gets too long and overwhelming, so self-care and self-assessment go by the wayside. But anytime we forget why we are on an entrepreneurial path, we are likely setting ourselves up for problems. These may manifest in poor health, broken friendships or families, even problems with your organization. These are messages that you need to step back and

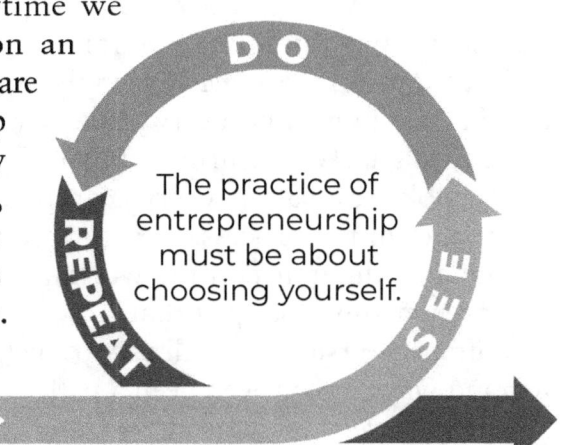

The practice of entrepreneurship must be about choosing yourself.

choose yourself. In the practice of entrepreneurship, choosing yourself must come first. Like the oxygen mask on an airplane, if you don't put on yours first, you will not be available to address the challenges you are facing.

PRACTICE: CHOOSE YOURSELF

Regardless of where you are on your own entrepreneurial journey, you may find the companion guidebook and *The See, Do, Repeat Competency Assessment©* to be useful self-awareness tools. (Visit: see-do-repeat.com.).

The companion guidebook and assessment can also help you as you think about how to build a team and surround yourself with people, who can help fill in the gaps. The practice of entrepreneurship doesn't require perfection and it doesn't require mastery. You don't have to, nor should you expect to, master every competency or skill in the See, Do, Repeat model right away. In fact, you may never master them all. That is okay. That is why most successful entrepreneurs have learned the power of surrounding themselves with good people.

Entrepreneurship is not a solo endeavor, even if you are a freelance solopreneur. You don't have to go it alone. Nor should you try. While some might find it useful to have a partner, you don't have to have a partner to benefit from the power of teamwork in your entrepreneurial endeavors. But surrounding yourself with the right people on your journey starts with self-awareness.

Intention and the advice to simply begin might seem like a big leap. In fact, it might be a very big leap for you. The constraints in your life might seem insurmountable. The entrepreneurial stories in this book are all about everyday people who did extraordinary things and, in the process, transformed not only their lives but also made a difference in the world around them. Every act of entrepreneurship does just that.

Entrepreneurship is a pathway to a better life in small ways and in grand ways. It has even been a pathway to overcome personal addiction, poverty, significant loss, and countless other extremely challenging circumstances. As one of my mentors, the late Dr. Jeffry Timmons, said "More than ever we are convinced that the creation and liberation of human energy through entrepreneurship is the single largest transformational force on the planet today."[38]

Regardless of where you are right now, the See, Do, Repeat model is available to you on some level. I hope you will consider the power of entrepreneurial practice in your life.

ENDNOTES

1   C.S. Dweck, *Mindset: The New Psychology of Success* (Random House Digital, Inc., 2008).

2   For example, see Fred Bramante and Rose Colby, *Off the Clock: Moving Education from Time to Competency* (2012) as well as M.J. Bradley, R.H Seidman, and S.R. Painchaud, *Saving Higher Education* for application.

3   To listen to some of those interviews, please subscribe to the *EnFactor Podcast* or visit https://www.enfactorpodcast.com/.

4   M. Casson, *The Entrepreneur: An Economic Theory* (Totowa, NJ: Barnes & Noble Books, 1982).

5   Shane, S., & Venkataraman, S. (2000). The promise of entrepreneurship as a field of research. *Academy of management review*, 25(1), p 220.

6   Matthias Filser, Victor Tiberius, Sascha Kraus, Tanita Zeitlhofer, Norbert Kailer, and Adrian Müller, "Opportunity recognition: Conversational foundations and pathways ahead," *Entrepreneurship Research Journal* (pre-published, 2020). https://doi.org/10.1515/erj-2020-0124

7   J.A. Schumpeter, *The Theory of Economic Development: An Inquiry into Profits, Capital, Credit, Interest, and the Business Cycle* (New Brunswick: Transaction Publishers, 1934).

8   While Schumpter borrowed this term from Warner Sombart and Karl Marx, he was not referring to the negative aspects of capitalism but instead to the positive and continuous improvement that is provided via entrepreneurship and capitalism.

9   I.M. Kirzner, *Competition and Entrepreneurship* (Chicago and London: University of Chicago Press, 1973).

10 Robert A. Baron, "Opportunity Recognition as Pattern Recognition: How Entrepreneurs 'Connect the Dots' to Identify New Business Opportunities," *Academy of Management Perspectives* (February 1, 2006). https://doi.org/10.5465/amp.2006.19873412

11 For more on this process, listen to Frans Johansson talk on the *EnFactor Podcast* about removing associative barriers).

12 Marc G. Berman, John Jonides, and Stephen Kaplan, "The Cognitive Benefits of Interacting with Nature," *Psychological* Science 19, no. 12 (December 1, 2008). https://journals.sagepub.com/doi/10.1111/j.1467-9280.2008.02225.x

13 James Webb Young, *A Tehcnique for Producing Ideas* (New York: McGraw-Hill, 2007)

14 Mihaly Csikszentmihalyi, *Creativity: Flow and the Psychology of Discovery and Invention* (New York: HarperPerennial, 1997).

15 For more on design methodology, consider books by Tom Kelly and/or Tim Brown, both of IDEO.

16 See https://youtu.be/5MeViSkg53s for a video describing Tembo. (The video was also produced by AJ Favicchio, another University of Tampa student who is now a successful videographer in LA.)

17 For more about the company see https://www.temboeducationgroup.com/.

18 For more on lean startup, consider Eric Ries, *The Lean Startup: How Today's Entrepreneurs Use Continuous Innovation to Create Radically Successful Businesses* (Currency, 2011) as well as Steve Blank and Bob Dorf, *The Startup Owner's Manual: The Step-By-Step Guide for Building a Great Company* (John Wiley & Sons, 2020).

19 C. L. Park and S. Folkman, "Meaning in the Context of Stress and Coping," *Review of General Psychology* 1, no. 2 (1997), 115–144. https://doi.org/10.1037/1089-2680.1.2.115

20 A. Bandura, "Self Efficacy," *The Corsini Encyclopedia of Psychology* (January 30, 2010), 1–3. https://doi.org/10.1002/9780470479216.corpsy0836

21 C. Dawson, D. de Meza, A. Henley, and G. R. Arabsheibani, "Entrepreneurship: Cause and Consequence of Financial Optimism," *Journal of Economics & Management Strategy* 23, no. 4 (2014), 717–742. https://doi.org/10.1111/jems.12076

22 J. S. Brown, A. Collins, and P. Duguid, "Situated Cognition and the Culture of Learning," *Educational Researcher* 18, no. 1 (1989), 32–42. https://doi.org/10.3102/0013189X018001032

23 According to Guy Kawasaki, one of the Apple employees originally responsible for marketing their Macintosh computer line in 1984 and author of *The Art of the Start*, the most powerful vision can be reduced to a mantra, a brief, memorable, and emotion-packed statement that the entire team can rally around.

24 Access the *See, Do, Repeat* reader's discount to take the EMP by visiting emindsetprofile.com/rebecca-white and entering code **SDR**.

25 I. C. Chadwick, and J. L. Raver, "Psychological Resilience and Its Downstream Effects for Business Survival in Nascent Entrepreneurship," *Entrepreneurship Theory and Practice* 44, no. 2 (2018), 233–255. https://doi.org/10.1177/1042258718801597

26 For more on the Barefoot Wine story, visit https://thebarefootspirit.com/ and read *The Barefoot Spirit: How Hardship, Hustle, and Heart Built America's #1 Wine Brand* by Michael Houlihan and Bonnie Harvey.

27 S. A. Sandage, *Born Losers*. (Harvard University Press, 2009), 4–5.

28 J. R. Mitchell and D. A. Shepherd, "To Thine Own Self Be True: Images of Self, Images of Opportunity, and Entrepreneurial Action," *Journal of Business Venturing* 25, no. 1 (2010), 138–154. https://doi.org/10.1016/j.jbusvent.2008.08.001

29 For a review of the literature, see Frederick G. Crane and Erinn C. Crane, "Dispositional Optimism and Entrepreneurial Success," *The Psychologist-Manager Journal* 10, no.1 (2007), 13–25. https://doi.org/10.1080/10887150709336610

30 For example, see G. Cassar, "Are Individuals Entering Self-Employment Overly Optimistic? An Empirical Test of Plans and Projections on Nascent Entrepreneur Expectations," *Strategic Management Journal* 31, no. 8 (2010), 822–840. https://doi.org/10.1002/smj.833

31 D.D. Meza, and C. Southey, "The Borrower's Curse: Optimism, Finance, and Entrepreneurship," *The Economic Journal* 106, no. 435 (1996), 375–386. https://doi.org/10.2307/2235253

32 T. Sharot, A. M. Riccardi, C. M. Raio, and E. A. Phelps, "Neural Mechanisms Mediating Optimism Bias," *Nature* 450, no. 7166 (2007), 102–105. https://doi.org/10.1038/nature06280

33 L. Rigotti, M. Ryan, and R. Vaithianathan, "Optimism and Firm Formation," *Econ Theory* 46, no. 1 (2011), 1–38. https://doi.org/10.1007/s00199-009-0501-x

34 A.C. Cooper, C. Y. Woo, and W. C. Dunkelberg, "Entrepreneurs' Perceived Chances for Success," *Journal of Business Venturing* 3, no. 2 (1998), 97–108. https://doi.org/10.1016/0883-9026(88)90020-1

35 See the work of Martin Seligman for example.

36 First introduced by Dr. Albert Ellis and then adapted by Dr. Martin Seligman.

37 Z. Lashani, M. R. Shaeiri, M.A. Asghari-Moghadam, and M. Golzari, "Effect of Gratitude Strategies on Positive Affectivity, Happiness, and Optimism," *Iranian Journal of Psychiatry and Clinical Psychology* 18, no. 2 (2012), 157–166. http://ijpcp.iums.ac.ir/article-1-1614-en.html

38 Jeffry A. Timmons and Stephen Spinelli, *New Venture Creation: Entrepreneurship for the 21st Century* (Boston, MA: McGraw-Hill, 2004), p.10.

ACKNOWLEDGMENTS

With Gratitude...

Thank you to the entrepreneurs, students and my colleagues in the entrepreneurship education discipline who have inspired me and my work over many decades. It has been an honor to be a part of your entrepreneurial journey. I am especially grateful to those of you whose stories I shared in this book.

Thank you to Jessica (not Jessie ☺) Leigh photos. And, James Z. – from toothbrushes and coffee lights to managing technology – you are always there when I need you and you manage to stay on top of it all. To Ramon Bosquez, for your very early input on the manuscript. Thank you for your honest and frank feedback. To Indraja Vaddadi, Emily Bagan, Dan Holohan, Bert Seither, Logan Higuera - thank you for you for your input on this book.

Family is everything to me. To my two amazing children, Bru and Caitlin, and three beautiful grandchildren, Harrison, Winter and Leo – thank you for making life fun and for giving me the motivation to make the world a better place every day. And to my parents, James and Betty, thank you for giving me life and for everything that I am and have. Even though you are not with me physically now, I hear your words and feel your love every day. I love all of you beyond words.

And, to my husband, Giles, my best friend and day to day life partner. Thank you for your steadfast love and support and for always being my greatest fan.

EN FACTOR

CONVERSATIONS WITH ENTREPRENEURS

Many of the stories I shared in this book have been inspired by the conversations I have had with guests on my podcast, En Factor™.

Their stories have provided me, and our listeners, with insight, action steps, and motivation towards perusing out entrepreneurial dreams.

To hear more first-hand stories of success, resilience through failure, and how to become a master in your field, please scan the QR code below or visit our website www.enfactorpodcast.com

Announcing the Sale of
Exploring The Practice of Entrepreneurship,
Based on the best selling book,
See, Do, Repeat: The Practice of Entrepreneurship.

Buy your copy today at

see-do-repeat.com

ABOUT THE AUTHOR

Rebecca J. White, Ph.D., is an award-winning educator, entrepreneur, and recognized global thought leader in entrepreneurship. She has developed nationally acclaimed entrepreneurship programs, founded multiple ventures, and contributed significantly to advancing entrepreneurial education.

Her work has earned numerous accolades, including the Karl Vesper Pioneer Award for Lifetime Achievement in Entrepreneurship, the Entrepreneurship Educator of the Year Award from the United States Association for Small Business and Entrepreneurship (USASBE), and recognition in 2019 as one of the Most Influential Board Members in the US by Women Inc. She has also been honored for her excellence in teaching, innovation, and mentorship.

Beyond academia, Dr. White has founded several businesses and advises entrepreneurs and organizations worldwide on innovation and value creation. Today she is Chairwoman of the board at MarineMax, she runs a successful podcast called En Factor: Conversations with Entrepreneurs, and she helps people around the world develop an entrepreneurial mindset and grow their businesses through the See Do Repeat Community found at drrebeccawhite.com.

A resident of Tampa Bay, Dr. White enjoys time with her family, exploring the waters aboard her boat, M/V Resilience, and embracing new adventures.

She can be reached at www.linkedin.com/in/drrebeccawhite and drrebeccawhite.com.